Beginning Ansible Concepts and Application

Provisioning, Configuring, and Managing Servers, Applications, and Their Dependencies

Shaun R Smith
Peter Membrey

Apress®

Beginning Ansible Concepts and Application: Provisioning, Configuring, and Managing Servers, Applications, and Their Dependencies

Shaun R Smith
Hong Kong, New Territories, Hong Kong

Peter Membrey
Kowloon, Hong Kong

ISBN-13 (pbk): 978-1-4842-8172-7
https://doi.org/10.1007/978-1-4842-8173-4

ISBN-13 (electronic): 978-1-4842-8173-4

Managing Director, Apress Media LLC: Welmoed Spahr
Acquisitions Editor: Aaron Black
Development Editor: James Markham
Coordinating Editor: Jessica Vakili

Distributed to the book trade worldwide by Springer Science+Business Media New York, 233 Spring Street, 6th Floor, New York, NY 10013. Phone 1-800-SPRINGER, fax (201) 348-4505, e-mail orders-ny@springer-sbm.com, or visit www.springeronline.com. Apress Media, LLC is a California LLC and the sole member (owner) is Springer Science + Business Media Finance Inc (SSBM Finance Inc). SSBM Finance Inc is a **Delaware** corporation.

For information on translations, please e-mail booktranslations@springernature.com; for reprint, paperback, or audio rights, please e-mail bookpermissions@springernature.com.

Apress titles may be purchased in bulk for academic, corporate, or promotional use. eBook versions and licenses are also available for most titles. For more information, reference our Print and eBook Bulk Sales web page at http://www.apress.com/bulk-sales.

Any source code or other supplementary material referenced by the author in this book is available to readers on the Github repository: https://github.com/Apress/Beginning-Ansible-Concepts-and-Application. For more detailed information, please visit http://www.apress.com/source-code.

Printed on acid-free paper

Table of Contents

About the Authors

Shaun R Smith is a Fellow of the British Computer Society (BCS) and holds degrees in Computer Science and Psychology. He has a wealth of experience across a broad range of technology, which he combines in novel ways to build out industry-leading, scalable and highly-secure solutions to complex problems. He evangelises simple, elegant and secure designs and these days is focusing on making the Internet a safer place to be and up-skilling the next generation.

Peter Membrey is a Chartered Fellow of the British Computer Society, a Chartered IT Professional and a Chartered Engineer with nearly a quarter of a century in the field. He has a doctorate in engineering and a masters degree in IT specialising in Information Security. He's co-authored over a dozen books, a number of research papers on a variety of topics and has recently been awarded the Distinguished Contributor award by the IEEE Computer Society.

These days he is focusing his efforts on creating a more private Internet, raising awareness of STEM and helping people to reach their potential in the field.

About the Technical Reviewer

Lambodar Ray is an IT team leader for public cloud transformation. He is skilled in IT infrastructure management focused on database systems, with diverse industry and business domain expertise in workforce management, expense management, procurement, and manufacturing shop floor automation. He is a Certified Oracle Cloud Architect Professional and AWS Architect Associate.

Introduction

This book is our attempt to help those who are new to the challenge of managing multiple servers and distributed applications. Most of us start off quite happily with a VM or two, and with a bit of help from Google, we manage to get things up and running. Usually, that means things are tweaked by hand with a little trial and error, but eventually all is well, and we are in production.

It may not happen right away, and it might not happen for a year, but at some point, sooner or later, something is going to go badly wrong, and you're going to have a crisis on your hands. Perhaps, you've already experienced the joy of sitting alone in the office at 4 a.m. with a stale cup of coffee (that sounds bad, but it beats being in a freezing cold server room), and that's why you've picked up this book. Perhaps, you've heard the horror stories and are adamant that you don't want any part of that. Or perhaps you think there just has to be a better way than doing this all by hand or writing lots of custom complicated scripts. You'd be right...

In this book, we will show you how to use Ansible to be able to build and manage servers and services in a simple and effective way. We will help you build your skills by introducing you to new techniques in each chapter that build on what you've learned before. This approach helps to make you immediately productive in the real world while still being able to explore and understand more complicated topics.

What Is Ansible?

At its heart, Ansible is a configuration management tool. These tools are now ubiquitous in modern computing environments, but although they actually had their beginnings in the 1950s at the US Department of Defense, it has taken a long time for them to be applied to computing environments. Until quite recently, configuration management was a rather manual process of checks and balances, with strict change management controls. These days, we've moved a few layers beyond this, where we describe the end state we require and allow the tools to figure out the best way to make that happen.

And this is where Ansible shines. Whether you're managing a single VM hosted in the cloud or 10,000 devices spread across the globe in physical data centers, Ansible can do it all.

Written in Python, with extensibility in mind, Ansible started with a few core modules for managing and configuring Linux servers. Thanks to the foresight and ingenuity of the developers, it has grown into a huge ecosystem capable of managing almost any system under the sun – from Linux and Windows servers, to routers and switches, to OpenShift and AWS services, and much much more. All with the same familiar syntax and ease of use you'll come to expect through your journey learning this amazingly flexible tool.

Having Ansible knowledge in your arsenal is more than just a nice to have. It's a critical skill on any developer's resume. It enables you to talk about various complex topics such as idempotence and declarative configuration, which we'll get into in the following chapters. It means you're able to automate your infrastructure and build it repeatedly. Many businesses, small and large alike, use Ansible in some way thanks to its simple syntax and the ability for it to be run from anywhere to anywhere without much overhead.

Unlike more traditional configuration management tools, which rely on constant communication between the controller and the hosts, Ansible does not. It can be run once only, or every day, by an individual, automation, or even many people on a team – it will always bring your hosts in line with the latest configuration. What's more, Ansible does not require the installation of a special piece of software called an "Agent" on the host that is being configured. This is a huge win for Ansible, since it enables the management of otherwise manually managed devices such as routers, switches, firewalls, and load balancers. It is also a huge win for those operating in a secure environment, where an Agent may introduce a new threat vector to their infrastructure. Ansible is different. It connects to hosts using the ubiquitous SSH, which in most cases will have already been locked down and closely monitored by any good security policy.

But Why Ansible?

That's a fair question. After all, Ansible is certainly not alone in the world of configuration management and administration. It is however one of the simplest tools out there. It has very minimal requirements on the target nodes in terms of requirements to run, and doesn't require an actual presence on the machine itself. This combined with the power that we can leverage from existing modules, custom inventories, and fact discovery (all things we cover later in the book), it really is a compelling choice for the needs of most people who need to get up and running quickly but have the room to expand.

Sounds Great – What Do We Cover?

Although this book is meant as a hands-on introduction to Ansible, we have taken a slightly different approach by building your skills up layer by layer and covering all the things we wished we knew when we were first navigating Ansible ourselves. Here's what we've got in store for you.

Chapter 1: Getting Setup and Running

As the title suggests, this chapter is all about getting you up and running with Ansible so that you can follow the exercises and examples throughout the rest of the book. We provide setup instructions for Linux, Windows, and Mac and briefly introduce Vagrant, an infrastructure tool that we'll use to build your Ansible environment.

Chapter 2: Your First Steps with Ansible

This is where you start finding your feet with Ansible. We'll cover how Ansible works and the principles and tools behind it. We'll then walk through a few different examples, each building on the last to get you up to speed on how Ansible looks and feels. After this chapter, you'll be able to run commands on remote systems and be able to build a basic inventory of hosts to manage.

Chapter 3: Choosing Your Targets

Now that you know how to execute some commands, it's time to show you how to target specific hosts and groups to execute them on. We show you how to augment your hosts file (to add crucial information such as an IP address and SSH port) and demonstrate how to use groups to make targeting multiple hosts a breeze. Sometimes, you're going to need to target groups and individual servers, and sometimes you're going to need groups of groups just to keep your inventory sane – don't worry, we cover both! We'll then wrap up the chapter with an alternative way of structuring your inventory that helps lay the foundations for greater flexibility.

Chapter 4: Your First Playbook

It's time to introduce playbooks, one of Ansible's core features. We recap modules and tasks and then jump into showing you how to create playbooks of your own. We cover each item step by step and build up the playbook over the chapter. We also touch on how to become root and the importance of an idempotent design.

Chapter 5: Batteries Included: Ansible Modules

Ansible modules are where its real power lies, and fortunately there are a huge selection of them already available for us to use. We'll talk about core modules and then provide an extensive walk-through of the apt module. Although fully featured and ideal for demonstration purposes, we quickly leave apt behind and demonstrate a small collection of additional modules that you're bound to find helpful. You'll get a feel for how Ansible manages to keep even disparate modules feeling similar and relatable.

Chapter 6: It's All Variable, That's a Fact!

Variables are an extremely powerful feature and can be set at many different levels in Ansible. Some variables might be set on individual hosts, but others may be on entire groups or perhaps set for a specific run. Knowing how to set there and which ones take precedence over others (spoiler alert, it isn't as obvious as you might hope) will let you get all the benefits of aligning your playbooks with the flexibility to handle a wide variety of real-world situations. We'll also cover the magic variables that always exist in Ansible and the concept of facts and fact gathering which allows us to build a repertoire of information on every host, a great source of variables to play with!

Chapter 7: Becoming an Ansible Jinja

So now that you can group and command your hosts and set key variables, it's time to see how this can actually be applied to configuration files and other content that you want to push to a server. If you've set a variable for a certain port in Ansible, you need a way to get that port information into your server's configuration file. This is where Jinja, a powerful (and often frustrating) templating engine, comes in. We'll show you how to use it to craft custom configuration files and show how to use flow control to either loop over items or skip them altogether. We also touch on how whitespace is handled which believe us has the ability to ruin your day!

Chapter 8: Handling Change

Handlers allow you to respond to events that happen as your playbook runs. They add flexibility and make writing particularly complex playbooks simpler by pulling out excess code. But how exactly do they work and when and why should they be used? That's the core of this chapter where we answer that and more!

Chapter 9: Roles: Ansible's Packing Cubes

Roles provide a way to group functionality and describe what's necessary for a particular host to deliver that functionality. We build upon the work you've already done (actually we end up moving or undoing most of it) and create the same end result but by using roles to group functionality instead. We'll also touch on role dependencies and setting variables at the role level, as well as a brief look at how legacy roles work and what you might see in production even though you won't create them that way yourself.

Chapter 10: Building a Load Balancer: Controlling Flow

So far, everything has been a relatively simple run of a playbook. Now we'll add some extra complexity to our setup to show you how to manage and control flow. We'll give an in-depth example with HAProxy to demonstrate the key features and use these enhancements to show how to use (and execute) tags.

Chapter 11: Running a Blog

In this chapter, we go all the way and set up a fully featured blog with all the trimmings. We introduce new modules, demonstrate how to create more complex configs, and show how to tie everything together in new roles. Pretty much everything you've learned so far is put to use in this chapter to give you a hands-on opportunity to try everything out.

Chapter 12: Locking Away Your Secrets: Vaults

Secrets are supposed to remain secret, and that's almost impossible if those secrets are ever stored on disk for everyone to see. We're big proponents of security, and so here we teach you all about Vaults, ansible's answer to storing secret information safely. Here, we store our SSL credentials (used for our web server) in an Ansible vault and show you how to decrypt and access it during the play itself.

Chapter 13: Worlds of Possibility

The final chapter is a roundup of all the awesome Ansible-related things that we couldn't fit into any of the existing chapters. Here, you'll find tools for dealing with AWS, with writing documentation (always a good thing!), finding great collections of preexisting (and often fully supported) modules that we can take advantage of, as well as where to look when you need some extra help.

Summary

We hope you have as much fun reading and working your way through this book as we had writing it. It's hands-on and moves quickly, but makes sure that it fills in the blanks as it goes. If you follow through each chapter, you'll definitely have a robust understanding of Ansible and be able to create high-quality playbooks that can add a lot of value both for your day-to-day work and for the teams of people that you have to work with.

So without further ado, let's jump straight into getting Ansible up and running!

CHAPTER 1

Getting Setup and Running

What We Will Cover

Before we get started and dive into Ansible, there are a few tools that you'll need to install, configure, and familiarize yourself with. That's because we will be building out an entire web stack right there on our computer. At this point, you may be thinking something along the lines of "why build a web stack ourselves?", followed closely by "why not build this on cloud infrastructure, such as AWS, GCP, Azure, etc.?".

Our answers are simple.

We primarily want to learn Ansible, and a great way of doing that is starting with simple foundations and building layer by layer on top until you have a functioning, working, and slightly complex stack. This is not a new way of building systems. Gall's law states that *a complex system that works is invariably found to have evolved from a simple system that worked* (John Gall, Systemantics: How Systems Work and Especially How They Fail).

Secondly, we want to address the cloud infrastructure question up front. We deliberately decided not to rely on any external resources for the following reasons:

© Shaun R Smith and Peter Membrey 2022
S. R. Smith and P. Membrey, *Beginning Ansible Concepts and Application*,
https://doi.org/10.1007/978-1-4842-8173-4_1

- Setup requires orchestration, and orchestration is what we're about to learn. We don't want to rely on too much up-front "just trust us it's correct" Ansible code to get started.

- External resources require free trials and/or payment. We'd rather not put anybody at a disadvantage by creating tasks that cost additional money (excluding access to a computer, of course).

That isn't to say Ansible cannot be used with all the above. It absolutely can manage all kinds of cloud services. But right now, we want to focus on learning *Ansible* – and for the most part keep the underlying infrastructure out of the way. With that in mind, let's walk through the minimal tools that we're going to get very familiar with throughout this book. Then we'll move on to installing and configuring them for your Ansible journey.

What You'll Be Using

An Internet Connection

Almost all the practical steps throughout this book will require access to a working Internet connection. That's because we will be managing servers. Although they will be virtual machines on our computer, we need to bootstrap our virtual machines with an operating system and install software, both of which predominantly come from online sources.

Virtual Machine Manager: VirtualBox

As we build up our infrastructure, we will have many servers performing different operations. They make up a reasonably resilient website-hosting stack. To facilitate this, we need to be able to create, boot, and manage virtual machines running the Linux operating system.

We opted for VirtualBox for a variety of reasons:

1. It is free of charge. One can simply download and install it from the website.

2. It is cross-platform. Whether you're running Windows, Linux, or using a Mac, there is a VirtualBox download for you.

3. It can be orchestrated by a useful tool named Vagrant, which we'll get to in a moment.

Why not Docker? We will be orchestrating these virtual machines using Ansible. The primary method for Ansible to reach into hosts is via SSH, and we will be configuring multiple services atop those hosts. Docker is simply not designed for such a use case. Again, that isn't to say you cannot use Ansible to orchestrate docker containers; but it isn't our goal.

Vagrant

Vagrant is a simple and powerful command-line tool which allows us to declare infrastructure setup in a single configuration file describing the virtual machine parameters (CPU, memory, network setup, etc.), operating system, and core package installation and configuration. It automates the initial operating system provisioning and allows us to build a production-like environment of multiple hosts which can be managed using simple commands. It is also cross-platform, working on Windows, Linux, and Mac.

This will be the top-level tool that you interact with directly. It abstracts the virtual machines away. We also use this to ensure a frictionless path to using Ansible tools, by creating a special virtual machine named controller, from which you can build and execute your Ansible environment regardless of the operating system running on your computer.

Ansible

Last, but certainly not least, we will be getting extremely familiar with Ansible. We will be running this within our environment, and it will be the application responsible for communicating with, configuring, and managing all the virtual machines in our setup.

Getting Setup

Without further ado, let's get started. These instructions will show screenshots using Windows, as the more popular platform; however, the instructions will also apply on Mac. For Linux users, we'll provide commands used for Ubuntu. If you are not using a Debian-based distribution, then please consult the project websites provided for installation instructions.

Downloading VirtualBox

Windows and Mac

Visit the VirtualBox website at `www.virtualbox.org/` and click the Download link on the left-hand side (see Figure 1-1).

VirtualBox

search...
Login   Preferences

Download VirtualBox

Here you will find links to VirtualBox binaries and its source code.

About

Screenshots

Downloads

Documentation

 End-user docs

 Technical docs

Contribute

Community

VirtualBox binaries

By downloading, you agree to the terms and conditions of the respective license.

If you're looking for the latest VirtualBox 6.0 packages, see VirtualBox 6.0 builds. Please also use version 6.0 if you need to run VMs with software virtualization, as this has been discontinued in 6.1. Version 6.0 will remain supported until July 2020.

If you're looking for the latest VirtualBox 5.2 packages, see VirtualBox 5.2 builds. Please also use version 5.2 if you still need support for 32-bit hosts, as this has been discontinued in 6.0. Version 5.2 will remain supported until July 2020.

VirtualBox 6.1.28 platform packages

- ⇨Windows hosts
- ⇨OS X hosts
- Linux distributions
- ⇨Solaris hosts
- ⇨Solaris 11 IPS hosts

The binaries are released under the terms of the GPL version 2.

See the changelog for what has changed.

***Figure 1-1.** Download page for VirtualBox*

From here, you will see a list of "platform packages" which are categorized by your host operating system. A host refers to the operating system that your computer is running. For Windows, choose "Windows hosts," or "OS X hosts" for Mac. Clicking the relevant host OS will immediately start the VirtualBox download to your computer.

At the time of writing, the latest version of VirtualBox is v6.1. We recommend always downloading the latest stable version of VirtualBox and keeping it up to date.

After the download has completed, you should work through the installation instructions. The default options are perfectly reasonable.

Partway through the installation process, you will be presented with the confirmation dialog in Figure 1-2. This is asking you to confirm installation of a device driver which enables the virtual machines to operate correctly. Ensure the Publisher is "Oracle Corporation" as in the screenshot and click "Install."

Figure 1-2. *Device driver installation dialog*

Installing VirtualBox will result in a short break in Internet connectivity, as it configures new network drivers for use with your virtual machines.

Once the installation has completed, you will be presented with a final screen asking if you'd like to run VirtualBox now (see Figure 1-3). You can uncheck that box before clicking "Finish," since there is no need to go into VirtualBox right now.

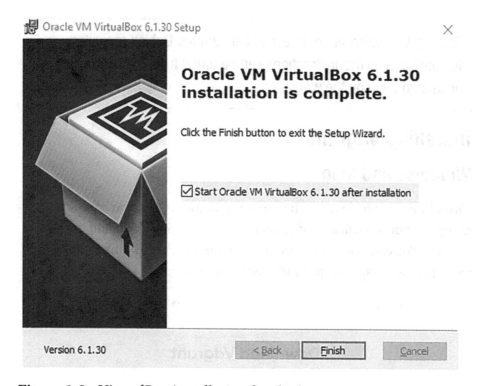

Figure 1-3. *VirtualBox installation finished*

Linux

From the download page in Figure 1-1, you can click "Linux distributions." From there, you will be presented with a list of supported Linux distributions. Simply click the relevant link and follow the instructions presented.

For Ubuntu, on clicking the link the Debian package .deb file will be downloaded to your computer. This can then be installed locally using

```
sudo apt install ~/Download/virtualbox-*.deb
```

To keep VirtualBox up to date, you can add the Debian repository to your sources list. Instructions can be found from the main Linux download page on the website.

Installing Vagrant

Windows and Mac

VirtualBox must be installed before using Vagrant. Once you have completed the installation of VirtualBox, you can download and install Vagrant. You can download it by clicking the "Download" link from their website at www.vagrantup.com/ – see Figure 1-4.

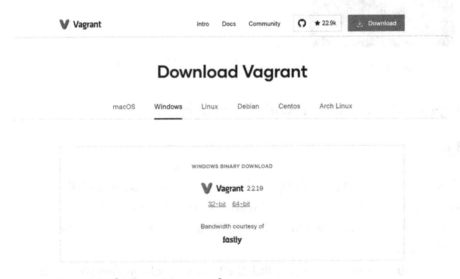

Figure 1-4. HashiCorp Vagrant home page

At the time of writing, the latest version of Vagrant is 2.2.19 as seen in Figure 1-4; however, we recommend you always download the latest stable release and keep it up to date to benefit from the latest security, features, and interoperability. Be sure to download the correct version for your computer; often, this will be 64-bit, but some readers may still be using 32-bit Windows.

If you're unsure whether you're running 32- or 64-bit Windows, you can find out by searching for "About your PC" and referring to System type.

As with VirtualBox, the Vagrant installation process is quite straightforward, and the default options are reasonable. Once completed, you will be prompted to restart your computer. You must do this before being able to use Vagrant.

Linux

To install the latest version of Vagrant on Debian-based Linux distributions, which include Ubuntu, you should navigate to the tab labeled Debian as seen in Figure 1-4.

From there, you will need to select either the 32-bit or 64-bit package. If you're unsure which version you're running, then you can find out using the following simple command:

```
$ lscpu
Architecture:              x86_64
CPU op-mode(s):            32-bit, 64-bit
Byte Order:                Little Endian
```

If you see x86_64 and 64-bit listed as shown earlier, then you should use the 64-bit installation package. If on the other hand you only see 32-bit listed, you will need to use the 32-bit package.

After downloading the Debian package, you can install it using

```
sudo apt install ~/Download/vagrant-*.deb
```

To keep Vagrant up to date, you can add the Debian repository to your sources list. Instructions can be found on the Linux tab of the website.

Setting Up Ansible

To bootstrap your virtual machine environment, we recommend you download the prebuilt `Vagrantfile` from the source Git repository. You will find this file in the root of the repository:

chapter_01	chapter_05	chapter_09	**Vagrantfile**
chapter_02	chapter_06	chapter_10	
chapter_03	chapter_07	chapter_11	
chapter_04	chapter_08	chapter_12	

To use Vagrant, you will need to open a terminal. For Linux users, this will vary depending on your distribution, but often searching for the term *Terminal* in your apps will usually work.

For Windows users, you can find the terminal by following these instructions:

1. Click the Start/Windows menu.

2. Start typing the word *Command Prompt* until you see the app "Command Prompt."

3. Click the app's icon.

You will now need to browse to where you downloaded the source files using the *cd* command. For example, if you saved that directory to your user's Downloads folder, this would be

```
> cd C:\Users\[username]\Downloads\beginning_ansible\
```

For Linux or Mac users, you would need to use forward slashes rather than backslashes, and the location of the downloaded files would differ.

Once in the correct directory, you can simply bring up the virtual environment by running the vagrant up command.

Throughout this process, you will need to grant permission for Vagrant to make changes to your computer using the VirtualBox interface. This is expected and must be allowed.

```
> vagrant up

Bringing machine 'controller' up with 'virtualbox' provider...
Bringing machine 'web-001' up with 'virtualbox' provider...
Bringing machine 'web-002' up with 'virtualbox' provider...
Bringing machine 'lb-001' up with 'virtualbox' provider...
Bringing machine 'db-001' up with 'virtualbox' provider...
```

This will take a few minutes. On the first run, you will see some messages about the Box "ubuntu/focal" not being found. That is ok; vagrant will automatically download the relevant files from the Internet to get you started.

Troubleshooting VirtualBox Errors

When attempting to first bring up the virtual machine environment, you might receive the following cryptic error message:

```
Stderr: VBoxManage.exe: error: Not in a hypervisor partition
(HVP=0) (VERR_NEM_NOT_AVAILABLE).
VBoxManage.exe: error: VT-x is disabled in the BIOS for all CPU
modes (VERR_VMX_MSR_ALL_VMX_DISABLED)
VBoxManage.exe: error: Details: code E_FAIL (0x80004005),
component ConsoleWrap, interface IConsole
```

This error is telling you that virtualization has not been enabled for your computer. To enable it, you would need to reboot into the BIOS (i.e., pressing a special key at boot time, such as DEL or F1) to enter the BIOS configuration screen. From there, you will need to enable virtualization. This is often under a section titled CPU and will often have the name Intel Virtualization Technologies, VT-x, or AMD-V. Specific instructions on how to achieve this vary from one manufacturer to the other, so we'd suggest searching for instructions online with a search term such as "Enable hardware virtualization [computer model]" (replacing computer model with the brand and model of your computer).

Using the Vagrant Environment

Status

To confirm the status of all vagrant-managed virtual machines:

```
> vagrant status
```

You will note that one of these VMs is called controller. We have provided this as a standard Linux machine with Ansible installed to ease the setup and installation instructions and provide a consistent environment for readers of this book. If you are comfortable and prefer to do so, you could delete the controller VM and simply set up Ansible directly on your own machine. Instructions on how to do so vary by operating system but can be found on the Ansible website here: https://docs.ansible.com/ansible/latest/installation_guide.

When starting up the virtual machines, you may see an error like this:

Release file for <> is not valid yet. Updates for this repository will not be applied.

That usually happens when you're using WSL2 on a laptop, because time drifts while the laptop is sleeping. To resolve the issue, one can simply run the following command to sync the time back from the hardware clock, from inside the WSL2 machine:

```
sudo hwclock -s
```

Logging In

Once you have the virtual machine environment running via Vagrant, it's time to log in and get familiar with your tools. It is possible to log in to any of the VMs that are managed by vagrant using special vagrant commands – so there is no need for any additional tooling at this point, simply

```
> vagrant ssh controller
```

You will then be dropped into the shell of the controller machine. You can confirm this by looking at the hostname in the prompt. Try to run ansible and ensure it is working as expected:

```
vagrant@ansible-controller:~$
vagrant@ansible-controller:~$ ansible --version
ansible 2.9.6
  config file = /etc/ansible/ansible.cfg
  configured module search path = ['/home/vagrant/.ansible/
  plugins/modules', '/usr/share/ansible/plugins/modules']
  ansible python module location = /usr/lib/python3/
  dist-packages/ansible
```

```
executable location = /usr/bin/ansible
python version = 3.8.10 (default, Sep 28 2021, 16:10:42)
[GCC 9.3.0]
```

To exit back out to your workstation, you can either type the word exit, followed by the Enter key, or press the key combination ctrl+d.

```
vagrant@ansible-controller:~$ exit [enter]
logout
Connection to 127.0.0.1 closed.

>
```

You can get into any of the virtual machines by repeating the preceding commands, replacing the name controller with another machine name, such as web-001.

Suspending the Virtual Environment

When you're not using the virtual environment, it is best to shut down the virtual machines. This saves your computer resources and battery (on a laptop). To do so, we will halt the machines, but not destroy them. Halt being similar to shutting down your laptop, you are able to boot them back up again quickly. Destroying on the other hand removes the files and VM entirely, meaning you'll have a long setup process the next time you wish to use them.

To halt all of the virtual machines, simply

```
> vagrant halt
```

If you'd like to halt only some of the VMs, you can simply pass the name of the target VM to this command:

```
> vagrant halt controller
```

For help using Vagrant or more advanced topics, please see their extensive documentation at www.vagrantup.com/docs.

Using Your Own Environment

Of course, you don't have to use the virtual environment provided. You could spin up Ubuntu Linux hosts on any cloud compute platform such as AWS, Google Cloud, or Azure.

To ensure a smooth process using this book, you should ensure that the nodes that you use conform to the following requirements:

- At least 4GiB RAM

- Running Ubuntu 20.04 (Focal)

- Public network access with SSH allowed from your workstation

- The following packages installed: python3-minimal python3-apt

You will use a total of four nodes throughout this book:

- 1x database server

- 1x load balancer server (we will configure this ourselves, not using a cloud-provided LB such as ELB)

- 2x web servers to simulate redundancy

You will need to substitute the IP addresses or hostnames for your target nodes any time we are discussing inventory files, accessing the web page that has been deployed or other commands that need to communicate directly with your nodes.

CHAPTER 2

Your First Steps with Ansible

Climbing into the Driving Seat

Shaun remembers the start of his journey, being thrown in the deep end at a new job and abruptly passed a production system that had been developed in this up-and-coming new tool that nobody could quite remember the name of; seemingly nobody knew what it did either – the person responsible had left. The only certainty was that it was responsible for building all new production systems and had numerous layers of magical scripts that "hid" this supposedly great new tool from view. There was no testing environment, and nobody had ever run it against an already-provisioned server, meaning it was not clear if production changes might break something critical in the near future. The skepticism was building fast.

That skepticism did not last long. Having peeled away layer after layer of obfuscation that had been added around this grand new application, what was discovered was a super simple, elegant tool with great potential. That tool was Ansible. Wading through the codebase, it was quickly apparent that Ansible had been massively misunderstood. It had been used to migrate from a solution whereby engineers copied a series of

© Shaun R Smith and Peter Membrey 2022
S. R. Smith and P. Membrey, *Beginning Ansible Concepts and Application*,
https://doi.org/10.1007/978-1-4842-8173-4_2

bash scripts to a host and executed them one by one to one where Ansible copied a series of bash scripts to a host and executed them in parallel – meaning Ansible was being used simply as a wrapper to push some old bash scripts to hosts and run them. Not much had changed at all.

Declare Your Intent

Ansible's *true* power, which had been so misunderstood, comes from using a declarative model. Traditionally, when using scripts to provision a host, you would define a series of commands that are executed in sequence. Those commands were designed to change some configuration or install some application. This is essentially an algorithm describing the "how" behind provisioning a host, such as "run this command to install application X, delete file Y," etc. There was often an inherent assumption that such a script would be run exactly once, at the time the host was provisioned. Running it a second time would be unchartered and dangerous territory since it might overwrite existing configuration or mutate the same thing a second time with unknown consequences. Add to that they would often only work against a particular operating system (OS) or even specific version of that OS.

Ansible's declarative model by contrast would specify the end state that you want the host to be in. You are describing "what" to achieve while leaving the "how" – the specific commands and steps to take to get there – to the interpretation of Ansible. A good example would be configuring an IP address on a network interface. Traditionally, you might run a series of Linux-specific *ifconfig* and *route* commands to set up the IP address, netmask, gateway, and default routes, along with a command such as *sed, or worse simply appending* the new configuration to a file, such that it is available after a reboot. Running those commands twice might result in the configuration appearing twice in the config file – at best resulting in an invalid configuration file. At worst, you might break your host's connectivity completely.

Conversely, in a declarative model you would describe the end state for those attributes in a structured format such as what the interface name, IP address, and gateway should look like, and Ansible would determine and execute only the specific commands required to get the host into that state. When your declaration is generic, and not using platform-specific commands, it can also be applied cross-platform on Linux, Windows, or Mac. The same "end state" definition would work for all. Additionally, if the host were already in the defined state, Ansible would take no action at all – avoiding those unintended side effects described earlier. The fact that Ansible will take no action if the desired state already exists means that it can be run against the same host multiple times, without side effects – great for keeping thousands of hosts' configuration in sync, especially where the configuration changes often.

This important concept is known as *idempotence*.

It Uses SSH

Another of Ansible's special powers was the decision to do all of this over an existing, tried and tested, secure protocol known as SSH (Secure Shell). Commonly used for administrators to gain remote access to devices such as routers, switches, firewalls, and servers, Ansible's use of SSH provides immediate benefits over other configuration management tools.

First, it can manage almost any device. SSH is the industry standard for remote access to devices. As almost every device managed by engineers in the wild today already includes SSH access, Ansible immediately gains interoperability with those devices. Contrast this with the traditional agent-based approach, whereby one must install a special piece of software on each device (known as an agent) to use the configuration management tool. Now you are immediately limited by the vendor creating an agent for your favored platform, something that is not going to happen for many esoteric and even some mainstream devices.

Second, SSH is tried and tested. It is a secure protocol, and its implementation is well known and open sourced. There is no new security risk introduced by Ansible. There are no agents listening to traffic from the Internet, and there are no new services running as an administrative user on your servers.

Harnessing This Power

Knowing all of this, we can start to understand why it was important for Shaun to migrate every step within those bash scripts mentioned earlier to declarative Ansible tasks – gaining consistency, idempotence, and readability into the entire provisioning process along the way. Before long, the entire provisioning tool had been overhauled, and the whole company was learning Ansible together. Engineers were empowered; there was no longer a shadowy domain where configuration management happened, and there were no magic scripts – it was out in the open (or in this case, Git) for all to improve – even nonprogrammers could read and understand this new declarative syntax.

Ansible was the tool that moved the management of 1000s of servers from a select few experts to decentralized management through simple code changes by developers. It made managing 1000 hosts almost as painless as managing just one.

What Changed?

The traditional model from the early 2000s saw experts using complex tooling such as PXE boot (for booting a computer entirely via a network connection rather than an operating system on the disk) often maintained by a network engineering team as it was tightly coupled with DHCP (a protocol for IP address assignment on a network), paired with a tool for automated, or unattended, installation of an operating system maintained by a Linux engineering team. These tools are often tied to a specific operating system such as Kickstart for Red Hat based and Preseed for Debian based – a huge overhead for environments that used multiple different operating systems. Kickstart or Preseed scripts defining an initial operating system configuration could be maintained by a team of people; it might be version controlled in predecessors to Git. Those configurations in turn would often define the installation and configuration of a small "agent" application on each host, responsible for communicating with a central server to pick up its running service configuration and software updates. Often, the configuration management tool would have its own dedicated team to manage it.

Maintaining network switch and router configurations to then ensure those hosts were connected to the correct network(s) would often fall to another team of specialized experts manually managing configurations via TFTP (Trivial File Transfer Protocol) triggered from SSH (Secure Shell) commands. Standardizing configuration through templates was manual effort, often by copying special template files and manually editing them. Needless to say, this was error-prone and not overly secure.

Thus, completing the journey from "needing a new service" to "service is up and running" went through many hoops and multiple team dependencies, each of these teams creating their own tooling, methods, and mistakes.

Contrast this with the model afforded by tools like Ansible, whereby all levels of engineers are able to configure 1000s of heterogeneous devices, distributed around the world, by pushing a code change to a version-controlled repository such as Git. We might configure the network, OS, install web server software, and set up load balancers – all in a single code change.

Here was a tool that could do it all. It was declarative, making it approachable and maintainable. It was idempotent, bringing more consistency and reliability. It was code, meaning it could be version controlled and peer reviewed. It used standard tools like SSH and didn't require installation of any agents on the device, meaning it could manage switches, firewalls, SaaS services, Linux hosts, Windows hosts, and everything in between. Being based on SSH meant it had a tried and tested security model – you didn't need to "trust" an agent, since you already trust SSH. Systems administrators were empowered.

This is the age of infrastructure as code (IaC).

Start Your Engines

Before going any further, make sure you have started the Vagrant environment that we built in Chapter 1 (or otherwise have Ansible installed with some VMs that you can target). We strongly recommend following along in the vagrant environment for ease of use.

Start all the vagrant hosts by issuing the following command:

```
> vagrant up
```

Now SSH into the ansible-controller VM with

```
> vagrant ssh controller
Last login: [date] from [ip]
vagrant@ansible-controller:~$
```

```
> cd /vagrant/
```

You should be dropped into a shell on the host named ansible-controller. From here, you need to use the cd command to move into the /vagrant/ directory. That is where you will conduct your work from.

Familiarize with the Controls

First things first, let's look at the ansible command. This is the most basic command in your arsenal – you'll often see it described as the "ad hoc" command, since it is primarily used to run ad hoc or one-off commands to gather information or perform some simple action on one or more of your hosts.

Imagine you are sending photos from your phone to your computer. One way of achieving this would be to browse your photos, select a single photo, hit send, and wait for that photo to be sent to your computer. Then proceed to the second photo and repeat. If you only have a single photo, this is fine – if it takes 5 seconds to copy a photo, and we only have one photo, it always takes 5 seconds. But what if you have 100 photos? Now it takes 500 seconds, or 8 minutes. Instead, what we would do is select all those 100 photos in one go, hit send, and wait for all 100 photos to be sent to your computer. This might take just 20 seconds, saving you a lot of time and clicking. To improve this process even more, you would want to automate it – meaning that when you plug the phone into your computer, some application runs that automatically syncs the latest photos from the phone to the computer, without you having to do much at all.

If the first example is equivalent to traditionally SSH'ing to a server and executing a command, repeating for all servers in your fleet – slow and error-prone – then parallelizing that command execution would be an ansible ad hoc command. Ansible can run the same command against 100s or 1000s of servers in parallel and show you the result. Meanwhile, ansible-playbook, which we'll get to later, would be like the automatic syncing – it can automate entire workflows (multiple steps that form a process) and execute them time and again against 100s or 1000s of servers.

But let's not get ahead of ourselves. First, we'll explore the ansible command in your controller environment:

```
> ansible
Usage: ansible <host-pattern> [options]
Define and run a single task 'playbook' against a set of hosts
Options:
<truncated>

  --list-hosts outputs a list of matching hosts;
                does not execute anything else

<truncated>
```

Note   We have truncated the output as referred to by <truncated>. That is because there are many options listed. We are only displaying the information of interest, but on your screen, you will see much more.

The first line of output shows us that the ansible command is expecting us to pass it a *host pattern* and some *options*. The *host pattern* is required, as denoted by the angled brackets < >, and a set of *options* are optional, as denoted by the square brackets [ ].

That means we *must* have a host pattern which tells Ansible which host(s) we wish to target. Ansible refers to this as a *pattern*, rather than a hostname, as it supports a wide variety of powerful host-matching patterns, such as includes, excludes, ranges, and wildcards. We will dive deep into host patterns in Chapter 3: Choosing your Targets, but for now we will be using very simple host patterns to get a feel for Ansible.

Next up are options, which are *optional*. All available options are listed by the output from the preceding example command (truncated in this book), all beginning with either a single or double dash (-/--).

These options change the behavior of the ansible command, telling it what action you wish to take and how you'd like it to behave. Most have sensible defaults. Here, we will be covering only a few of the most used options.

Let's go ahead and tell ansible that we want to list all hosts available. We will do this by using *all* as a host pattern, meaning every host that ansible knows about, and the option *--list-hosts* which will output a list of all hosts matching the host pattern, without doing anything else:

```
> ansible all --list-hosts

[WARNING]: provided hosts list is empty, only localhost is
available. Note that the implicit localhost does not match 'all'

  hosts (0):
```

Oops, we got our first warning, but with a useful hint. We asked ansible to tell us of all the hosts it currently knows about – its response essentially says it doesn't know of any hosts yet (that makes sense, we haven't told it of any), except a mention of an implicit *localhost*.

A localhost will **always** exist in Ansible, and it refers to the host that you are currently working on – the ansible controller. This means that Ansible can *always* run tasks against the localhost without any special magic: something that will come in useful in a later chapter when we explore task delegation. While it always exists, you will not see it listed in the preceding hosts list. That is because the implicit *localhost*, being a special case, will never belong to any group.

But we *can* target it directly as a host pattern. Let's do that:

```
> ansible localhost --list-hosts

 [WARNING]: provided hosts list is empty, only localhost is
available. Note that the implicit localhost does not match 'all'

  hosts (1):
     localhost
```

That looks better. Now we have one host, *localhost*. We still received the warning – and will continue to do so, as we have not yet provided ansible with a host list. We will worry about that later.

Now let's do something useful with localhost. Let's run an ansible *module* against it. We will use a different option this time, -m, which tells ansible the *module* we would like to use. A module is responsible for one type of action against a host; in this case, let's use a module named *ping*. This is the most basic of ansible modules that loosely follows the concept of the popular ping command which exists on practically every networked system in the world:

```
> ansible localhost -m ping

 [WARNING]: provided hosts list is empty, only localhost is
available. Note that the implicit localhost does not match 'all'

localhost | SUCCESS => {
    "changed": false,
    "ping": "pong"
}
```

Let's break this down line by line to see what just happened.

```
localhost | SUCCESS => {
```

We ran a task against a host named *localhost*, and it was successful. Ansible has several outcomes for a task, the three major ones being SUCCESS, FAILED (tried, but failed to run the task), and UNREACHABLE (unable to talk to the host).

```
    "changed": false,
```

Ansible tasks may change something on the target host, for example, it may change a configuration file or restart a service. In this case, the ping module did not change anything on the host, and so changed is set to false.

```
    "ping": "pong"
```

We sent a ping, and the server replied with pong. There is much more to this than a simple reply though – this actually tells us that Ansible was able to talk to the host, it was able to log in using valid credentials, and it was able to execute a command against the host and gain a positive response. The ping module tells us that the host is in a state suitable to be managed by Ansible.

Ping is often replied to with pong, as in a game of ping-pong; however, the original intent behind the ping application's name was to mirror the "ping" sound of active sonar which emits a pulse of sound and listens for echoes to determine existence of objects, much like the tool itself.

More Than Ping: Our Hello World

Ping is fun, and we learned a little history along the way. But wouldn't it be even more fun if we learned something about the host we are targeting? As we mentioned earlier, ad hoc commands can be as simple as a shell command run against one or more hosts. In that vein, Ansible comes with a module conveniently called *shell*. The shell module, unlike ping, requires an *input* – a command to execute on the shell.

To pass an input into the module, we need to use another option, the *--args* or *-a* option (used interchangeably). Each module takes different inputs, and there is a specific format used for this – but for now let's focus on the shell module, whose input is simply the command you wish to execute on the shell of the target host.

We will use a shell command to tell us the hostname:

```
> ansible localhost -m shell -a hostname
```

[WARNING]: provided hosts list is empty, only localhost
is available. Note that the implicit localhost does not
match 'all'

```
localhost | SUCCESS | rc=0 >>
ansible-controller
```

As you can see, this output is slightly different. Each module may provide slightly different outputs – some with more information than others. Let's walk through this:

```
localhost | SUCCESS | rc=0 >>
```

Again, we ran a task against a host called localhost. That task was successful. But we also have an additional piece of information: rc=0. This is telling us the *return code* of the command that was run. A return code of zero almost always means the command executed without error. In fact, this is so standard that the Ansible shell module uses the return code to determine the SUCCESS/FAILED state by default.

```
ansible-controller
```

Finally, we are shown the output of the command. The Ansible shell module is returning the standard output (what you would have seen had you run this via SSH) of the command that was executed on the host – in this case, the output of the *hostname* command, which is the name of the host: ansible-controller.

Let's see the return code in action, with a failing task. For this, we will use the false command, which always exits with a nonzero return code. The documentation for the false command puts it very clearly: *do nothing, unsuccessfully*:

```
> ansible localhost -m shell -a false
localhost | FAILED | rc=1 >>
non-zero return code
```

Here, we can see that the task FAILED, with a nonzero return code of 1 (rc=1). We then get an error message from Ansible – this will often be the error output (stderr) of the command, but in this case false has no output, and so Ansible tells us why *it* decided to fail the task: *nonzero return code*.

Note   If you get stuck along the way, there are two main ways of getting help for applications on the command line. Those are ansible --help and man ansible. Both will describe all options available.

Get Moving: Making a Change

This is all well and good, but how does printing the hostname, or causing an error, help you better manage your hosts? What if we want to change something on the host?

One approach would be to simply use the shell module to perform your tasks. Going back to the hostname command, we could extend the command to not only tell us the hostname but to change it:

```
> ansible localhost -m shell -a "hostname new-name"

localhost | FAILED | rc=1 >>
hostname: you must be root to change the host name
non-zero return code
```

Well, that didn't quite go as expected. The ansible task FAILED with a return code of 1. However, the output gives some useful insight into why: *you must be root to change the host name.* This is quite common in the Linux world, with root being the admin user and us trying to change a system-wide configuration. Luckily, Ansible is designed for such environments, and we can quickly tell ansible in a declarative manner to "become" the admin user in order to run this task. We do so using another option --become or -b:

```
> ansible localhost -b -m shell -a "hostname new-name"
localhost | SUCCESS | rc=0 >>
```

That seems to have worked; let's verify:

```
> ansible localhost -m shell -a "hostname"

localhost | SUCCESS | rc=0 >>
new-name
```

Great – the hostname has been updated. But something doesn't quite feel right. Remember at the start of the chapter, Shaun was lamenting that people had misunderstood ansible and were using it to describe the "how" to get something done? That's exactly what we just did!

We told ansible to run the hostname command on the host, with a new hostname. Ansible will always run that command irrespective of what the hostname is already set to – just as instructed. That can have unintended consequences with more complicated tasks such as adding lines to files, where you repeat the same action multiple times. It is not idempotent.

Instead, we should be declarative – describing the end state that we expect the host to be in, without telling Ansible how to get there. It will then determine if any change is needed (perhaps, the host is already at that state) and what the best way of making that change is.

For example, our simple hostname change will only change the hostname while the host is running; it would be lost on reboot. Ansible modules understand these complexities and ensure all the boxes are checked.

Let's switch this around. Instead of describing the "how," we will instead use the hostname module and switch to the "what." We will be declarative:

```
> ansible localhost -b -m hostname -a "name=newer-name"
localhost | SUCCESS => {
    "ansible_facts": {
        "ansible_domain": "",
        "ansible_fqdn": "newer-name",
        "ansible_hostname": "newer-name",
        "ansible_nodename": "newer-name"
    },
    "changed": true,
    "name": "newer-name"
}
```

Wow – that is a lot more detailed output. What does it all mean?

```
    "ansible_facts": {
        "ansible_domain": "",
        "ansible_fqdn": "newer-name",
        "ansible_hostname": "newer-name",
        "ansible_nodename": "newer-name"
    },
```

This is something we will cover later. For now, consider ansible facts a set of key-value pairs that describe the environment and the host that ansible is currently targeting. They contain facts in the literal sense – such as the hostname, disk configuration, and network configuration of the host. In this case, ansible is presenting those related to the hostname that we have just changed.

```
    "changed": true,
    "name": "newer-name"
```

31

Now we see this changed value again, as with the ping module. Only this time changed is set to true, meaning a change was made on the target server. Ansible will only make a change if one is required to bring the server to the declared state – otherwise, no change will be made. That is the concept of idempotence in action. We then see the name that the hostname was changed to.

To show this concept, let's run the **exact** same command again:

```
> ansible localhost -b -m hostname -a "name=newer-name"

localhost | SUCCESS => {
    "ansible_facts": {
        "ansible_domain": "",
        "ansible_fqdn": "newer-name",
        "ansible_hostname": "newer-name",
        "ansible_nodename": "newer-name"
    },
    "changed": false,
    "name": "newer-name"
}
```

We ran the same command again, only this time ansible reported *changed* as *false* – no changes were made on the host, because no change was needed. The Ansible hostname module understands that the current state of the host matches the declared state in our command. It will not execute anything it doesn't need to.

Getting Help with Modules

All of the modules available in Ansible are very well documented both on their website and through a local command: *ansible-doc*. To understand the arguments that can be passed to a module, such as the hostname module where we gave an argument of name=hostname, you can read the module documentation with the following command:

```
> ansible-doc hostname

> HOSTNAME    (/usr/lib/python2.7/dist-packages/ansible/
modules/system/hostname.py)
```

Set system's hostname, supports most OSs/Distributions, including those using systemd. Note, this module does *NOT* modify `/etc/hosts'. You need to modify it yourself using other modules like template or replace. Windows, HP-UX and AIX are not currently supported.

OPTIONS (= is mandatory):

```
= name
        Name of the host
```

REQUIREMENTS: hostname

```
EXAMPLES:
- hostname:
        name: web01
```

You can see a detailed description of what this module does and which operating systems it supports. You can see a list of options; these are the arguments that we passed into our ansible command using the -a option. In this case, there is just one argument, name, and it is mandatory (denoted by the equals sign).

You can then see some information about the author, followed by examples of using the module. Note these examples are formatted in a way that would be used by a playbook – something we will get to later.

Working with Others: A Simple Inventory

We have been using ansible to target our local controller, localhost, which is a great way to learn the basics – but we need to branch out to truly understand the parallelization power that ansible brings us.

Let's target some remote hosts. Remember to ensure all of the vagrant hosts are up and running (see the section "Start Your Engines" at the beginning of this chapter).

First, we need to create a very basic version of what is called an inventory file. That is what ansible is referring to as the "host list" being empty when we use --list-hosts.

Go ahead and create a new file in your vagrant environment named hosts and add the following content (remember this can be on your local machine, in the vagrant directory, or inside the ansible-controller if you're comfortable with editors such as vim or nano):

```
web-001.local
```

Save the file and go back to your ansible-controller. We will now execute the --list-hosts command again to see if this is picked up. We will need to tell ansible where to find our new inventory file using another new option --inventory or -i (used interchangeably):

```
> ansible -i hosts all --list-hosts

  hosts (1):
    web-001.local
```

Ansible found the host. If that did not work for you, you should have been provided some warnings by Ansible. Common problems might be

1. You are not in the correct directory – cd /vagrant/.

2. You created the file in the wrong location – ls / vagrant to see if the *hosts* file exists.

Now that we have our remote host available to ansible, we will fire up the trusty ping module once again to ensure the host is reachable and ready to be managed by ansible:

```
> ansible -i hosts all -m ping
```

```
The authenticity of host 'web-001.local (192.168.98.111)' can't
be established.
ECDSA key fingerprint is SHA256:****.
Are you sure you want to continue connecting (yes/no/
[fingerprint])?
```

This message will happen exactly once the first time you connect to any host using Ansible. It is a security feature of the underlying SSH protocol used to talk to remote hosts. You can confirm by typing the word yes and pressing return, at which point execution will continue with the following output:

```
web-001.local | SUCCESS => {
    "changed": false,
    "ping": "pong"
}
```

Ansible just reached out to a remote host and received a reply. Moving from talking to localhost to a remote host really is as simple as telling ansible how to reach the target host in an inventory file. Any command you can run in ansible, you can now run against this remote host too!

To avoid having to confirm host keys while learning Ansible, you can create a new file named *ansible.cfg* and add the following content:

```
[defaults]
host_key_checking = false
```

But please do not do this when working with production systems, as it skips identification of the remote host and opens you up to potential man-in-the-middle attacks within your infrastructure.

Unleash the Power in Parallel

We have talked a lot about parallelization – having ansible perform a task against multiple hosts; but we haven't yet demonstrated that. To wrap up your first steps with Ansible, we will add a second host to the simple inventory file and target them both simultaneously.

Open the inventory file hosts that you created, and modify it:

```
web-001.local
web-002.local
```

Next, run that same ping command again, targeting all hosts:

```
> ansible -i hosts all -m ping
web-001.local | SUCCESS => {
    "changed": false,
    "ping": "pong"
}
web-002.local | SUCCESS => {
    "changed": false,
    "ping": "pong"
}
```

Ansible performed the ping against both hosts in our inventory file and returned a unique result for each of the hosts. The result for each host will be returned as the response arrives – some hosts may be faster than others, so these results will not always be presented in alphabetical order.

It is worth noting that Ansible by default will run against five hosts in parallel, which is great when we are dealing with just a few hosts – but when you start working with 100s or even 1000s of hosts, you will definitely want to increase this parallelization factor. Ansible refers to this as *forks*, and it is simply another option we can pass into the command (`--forks` or `-f`).

Plugging in the GPS

We now have our map telling Ansible where to find our hosts. Let's ensure it knows where to find that every time it's needed rather than having to add the `-i hosts` option to every command we execute. To do that, we will need to create or edit the configuration file named ansible.cfg in the current directory.

Under the heading [defaults], we need to add an option telling Ansible where it can find this new inventory file, like this:

```
[defaults]
inventory = hosts
```

Now, we can execute the same commands as before, but without needing to specify where to find the inventory file:

```
> ansible all -m ping

web-001.local | SUCCESS => {
    "changed": false,
    "ping": "pong"
}
web-002.local | SUCCESS => {
    "changed": false,
    "ping": "pong"
}
```

Summary

We covered a lot of ground in this chapter, especially in terms of Ansible concepts covering the whole gamut from declarative programming and idempotence to host lists and inventories. It's ok if those terms are still a little fuzzy; we will be referring to them throughout this book as they are so key to Ansible's wizardry.

We started off by introducing the ansible command – what inputs it requires (a required host pattern and optional options) and how to list the hosts that ansible is aware of. We discussed the implicit localhost and how, while it is always available (hence the term implicit), it will never be included in a group.

We then targeted the implicit localhost with our active sonar module, ping, and explored what it means for it to succeed. While ping is great, we strive for more. That's why we then used a second ansible module called shell – a way of directly issuing shell commands to the target host(s) via ansible. We showed how ansible interprets the return code to provide you with a clear SUCCESS/FAILED response and how it passes through the output of the command to your local controller machine.

While it's great that we can now run commands on the server to find out information, how about actually changing something? We learned that some changes require root access and that Ansible has a declarative way of signaling that using the *become* option. We then updated the hostname using the *shell* module, before realizing that is the imperative way of expressing the task – and what we should be doing is declaring the end state we expect the host to be in and letting Ansible perform its magic to make it so. We explored running the same module twice against the same server to show how the second run does not make any changes – it is idempotent.

We then wrapped up by creating a simple inventory file that now contains two hosts, and we ran our ping command against a remote host. We then explored running the command against multiple hosts in parallel to show how you might save yourself a lot of typing by using Ansible even for simple system administration tasks.

In the following chapter, we will deep dive into the inventory file as it is the central core of your Ansible world – it determines which servers are under your control and provides you mechanisms for managing groups of hosts effectively.

CHAPTER 3

Choosing Your Targets

In the previous chapter, we created what we called a very simple inventory file, so you could be forgiven for thinking it isn't all that important. Nothing could be further from the truth. The inventory file is pivotal to your Ansible journey, and mastering it is the key to effectively managing large, complex configurations of servers.

Imagine for a moment that you jump into the driving seat of your car, you've put your safety belt on, started the engine, checked the fuel level, and slowly pull away, starting out on your journey. But wait: Where are we going, and how exactly do we get there? We forgot two critically important pieces of information: the address and the map!

It's all well and good telling Ansible exactly what you want it to do to your servers, say "install the web server application nginx on the server I call web-001." But without the inventory, Ansible has no way to know that web-001 even exists or where it is (i.e., it doesn't have a hostname or an IP address) or how it should get there (i.e., SSH port, username, password) – it doesn't have a destination or a map.

You may be thinking: that's ok… I have a hostname already – I'll just tell Ansible to go there, and it doesn't need an inventory, just like I find my way to Disneyland using only the road signs. Well, perhaps – but Ansible is more like your terrified-to-be-on-the-road Aunt who will only set out with

© Shaun R Smith and Peter Membrey 2022
S. R. Smith and P. Membrey, *Beginning Ansible Concepts and Application*,
https://doi.org/10.1007/978-1-4842-8173-4_3

turn-by-turn instructions, and even then only on the roads she already knows well. Ansible requires that you define the inventory it should manage before it is willing to talk to your servers.

To make this point, let's give it a go. We'll tell Ansible to operate against an arbitrary hostname on the Internet and see how it reacts:

```
ansible google.com --list-hosts
```

```
[WARNING]: Could not match supplied host pattern, ignoring:
google.com
```

```
[WARNING]: No hosts matched, nothing to do
```

```
 hosts (0):
```

Just like Auntie when we said "let's go somewhere new," Ansible isn't even going to let us leave the house! Think of this as a safety measure, a kill switch. If the destination is not in the inventory, Ansible isn't even going to entertain talking to it. This is to protect you – to prevent you from getting lost and accidentally turning up at the wrong party or performing actions against a server you didn't intend to.

Note   We can work around this by specifying the full inventory on the command line with `-i "web-001,web-002"`, but that isn't the same as not creating an inventory – it is creating a temporary inventory.

To summarize: An inventory is **not optional**. The inventory is your map – it tells Ansible where to go (which servers you need to operate against) and how to get there (hostnames, IP addresses, usernames, SSH ports, etc.). Because it is such an important concept, we'll spend this entire chapter talking about the inventory and the many ways in which it can serve you.

Exploring Our Simple Inventory

Looking back at our inventory from the previous chapter, you'll see we added two hosts for Ansible to operate against:

```
web-001.local
web-002.local
```

Let's look once again at how we would use this in our ansible command:

```
> ansible all -m shell -a hostname
```

This all works because a few things are true:

1. We are logging in to the controller (where we run the ansible command) and both web-001.local and web-002.local servers with the same username: ***vagrant***.

2. web-001.local and web-002.local are valid DNS hostnames that are managed by Vagrant, and so we know where to reach those hosts without having to specify an IP address.

3. SSH connections to web-001.local and web-002. local are done via the standard port 22.

Ansible and the underlying SSH connection it uses choose sensible defaults, meaning we can take a lot of settings for granted. This is great in a controlled environment – but in the real world, often it is not the case.

What if we wanted to add a host, but this time there wasn't a valid hostname to use, or we need to log in using a different SSH port? Let's modify web-002.local to *not* be a valid hostname.

Modify the inventory file hosts, and make it look like this:

```
web-001.local
web-002
```

We removed the .local suffix from web-002, which is no longer a valid hostname. I wonder how Ansible will cope with knowing its destination, but not having any part of the map showing how to get there.

Let's run the same command again and find out:

```
> ansible all -m shell -a hostname
```

web-002 | UNREACHABLE! => {
    "changed": false,
    "msg": "Failed to connect to the host via ssh: ssh: **Could not resolve hostname web-002**: Temporary failure in name resolution\r\n",
    "unreachable": true
}

web-001.local | SUCCESS | rc=0 >>
web-001

Interesting. Ansible failed, but not immediately; we still got a successful result back for our original host web-001.local, while the second host web-002 presented an error. That's because Ansible operates on each of the hosts independently and is reporting back on the state of each host. Even when one or more hosts fail during an Ansible run, no other host's execution will be impacted, unless we explicitly tell Ansible to stop, but that is a topic for later.

Here is the full error message for web-002:

```
Failed to connect to the host via ssh: ssh: Could not resolve
hostname web-002: Temporary failure in name resolution
```

Ansible is telling us that it tried to find the host but was unable to. It assumed there was a failure in name resolution (meaning DNS on the controller failed), which makes sense knowing that the DNS name we provided is not valid. Sometimes, Ansible cannot give a more specific reason, as it has no way of knowing the difference between a failure to look up the name and the name simply not existing.

To fix this, we can give Ansible a map, telling it how to reach our host. Let's do that now; once again, modify hosts:

```
web-001.local
web-002 ansible_host=192.168.98.112 ansible_port=22
```

We have given Ansible an IP address at which to reach web-002. We have done so using what we call a **host variable** – a variable defined for a specific host in the inventory.

Now let's try that same command again:

```
> ansible all -m shell -a hostname

web-001.local | SUCCESS | rc=0 >>
web-001

web-002 | SUCCESS | rc=0 >>
web-002
```

Much better – Ansible can now reach both of our hosts, one using the fully qualified hostname and the other using a host *short name* as defined in the inventory along with an IP address directing Ansible how to get there. You can see the name shown for each of our hosts is exactly as it was written *in the inventory file* – this is known as the inventory_hostname. We can name a host anything we choose, so long as we tell Ansible how to reach the host. We could just as easily have called web-002 something entirely different, such as webby, if we so desired, and it would still connect using the IP address we specified.

A **host variable** appears in the inventory file on the same line as the hostname. The value is applied only to the specific host in question.

We can define absolutely any host variable we choose, separated by spaces, as can be seen with `ansible_host` and `ansible_port` earlier. We could give our web servers a host variable specifying the HTTP port that we want to appear inside a configuration file – we will touch on that more later. For now, let's take a look at some of the commonly used **built-in** host variables that modify Ansible's behavior:

ansible_host	The hostname or IP address to connect to
ansible_port	The SSH port to use when connecting to the host
ansible_user	The username to use when connecting to the host
ansible_become	When connecting to a host as an unprivileged (non-admin) user, become an admin user before executing commands

A More Complex Structure

Hopefully by this point, you have a clear grasp on how to define a new host in your Ansible inventory and how we can use simple host variables to inform Ansible how to connect to your hosts. Up to now, we have been targeting **all** hosts within our inventory, as evident in the command:

```
> ansible all -m shell -a hostname

      ^ the servers we are targeting
```

That is all well and good when we have one or two hosts, but what if we want to get smarter about how and when we run tasks against our hosts?

Perhaps, we have a variety of different host **types** such as web servers, load balancers, database servers – which we would like to be able to target independent of one another.

Luckily for us, the Ansible inventory supports **groups**, and they are extremely flexible. A group simply has a unique name and contains any number of hosts or even other groups – allowing us to slice and dice our inventory up any way we choose.

We can create a group with a simple line that is known in the world of INI files as a **header**. Ansible interprets these headers as "special lines" which are used to define the group name.

Let's go ahead and add a group to our inventory file, which will contain all our webservers. Once again, open your hosts file and add the following:

```
[webservers]
web-001.local
web-002 ansible_host=192.168.98.112
```

The important addition (in bold) is the **group name**. We know this because the name of the group (webservers) is surrounded by square brackets [ ] – a special syntax to create a group in Ansible. The group name can contain only letters, numbers, and underscores.

Now we have the new group, *webservers*, we can target it with any Ansible command instead of using the hostname or the keyword *all*. At this point, we want to introduce a very useful option for Ansible which will become your go-to option when working with complex groupings – it is always a good sanity check before running any Ansible playbook against production hosts, especially when managing 1000s of servers.

This is the **--list-hosts** option; let's take a look at what Ansible has to say about this option:

```
ansible --help

<truncated>

  --list-hosts  outputs a list of matching hosts;
                does not execute anything else
```

The keyword here is **matching hosts**. We can use this option before running an Ansible command to show a list of all hosts that **match** any combination of hostnames, groups, or other filtering we choose to do on our host list.

Let's use this to see how our new *webservers* group is looking:

```
ansible webservers --list-hosts
  hosts (2):
    web-001.local
    web-002
```

As you can see, the webservers group exists and contains two hosts, just as we would expect given the group that we created in our inventory file earlier. Those two servers, of course, will also still be a member of the **all** group, which includes all hosts in the inventory regardless of group membership:

```
ansible all --list-hosts
  hosts (2):
    web-001.local
    web-002
```

But you haven't proven anything, I hear you say. The *webservers* group and the *all* group are identical, so how do I know this group really is differentiating my hosts? Great question. Let's add a third host, a load balancer, to the inventory. For now, it doesn't matter what the load balancer is or why we need one – we are just getting familiar with the inventory file.

Open up the hosts file again, and add the following:

```
[webservers]
web-001.local
web-002 ansible_host=192.168.98.112

[load_balancers]
lb-001.local
```

Now we can start to see the power of groups. Let's run the preceding commands again to show how these groups really work. We'll start with the special **all** group, showing every host in our inventory:

```
ansible all --list-hosts
  hosts (3):
    lb-001.local
    web-001.local
    web-002
```

Great – we now have three hosts in our inventory, and *all* doesn't care about group membership, just as intended.

Now, let's target our web servers only:

```
ansible webservers --list-hosts
  hosts (2):
    web-001.local
    web-002
```

Beautiful – two hosts, web-001.local and web-002.
How about this new group, load_balancers?

```
ansible load_balancers --list-hosts
  hosts (1):
    lb-001.local
```

Perfect. You can start to see how simple groups can help manipulate the target of your Ansible tasks.

Groups are powerful, but they are not magical. Ansible is simply resolving the target group name that was passed into it and coming up with a single flat list of hosts to target, which is what you are seeing as the hosts list earlier. That is done at the start of every Ansible execution – and your commands will only ever be run against those matching hosts.

Combining Hosts and Groups

Groups are great, but sometimes you just want to target a couple of hosts from a larger group. Imagine over time you have built up many groups for various functions – you have web servers, load balancers, databases, application servers, and firewalls; and on top of that, you have a staging environment and a production environment.

Suddenly, using the **all** group isn't so appealing. But what if you still want to target just some of those groups – perhaps, you have some configuration change that you need to make only on the webservers and the load balancers.

Thankfully, you don't need to run Ansible multiple times. The host and group filtering that we used previously is actually much more powerful. There are many *patterns* that can be used to manipulate exactly which hosts from which groups we target.

The most basic form would be to target all hosts that belong to *either* webservers or load_balancers:

```
ansible webservers:load_balancers --list-hosts

  hosts (3):
    web-001.local
    web-002
    lb-001.local
```

We have achieved this by putting both group names, separated by a colon (:). You can think of the colon as a logical **OR** – meaning target all of the hosts from either the webservers groups OR the load_balancers group – you will end up with all hosts from both groups. This is supported with any combination of groups and hosts – we could just as easily target multiple hosts directly using this method:

```
ansible web-001.local:web-002 --list-hosts
```

```
  hosts (2):
    web-001.local
    web-002
```

Of course, targeting many hosts by name in this way would not be very efficient. There would be a lot of typing, and the chance of making mistakes is large. That is why Ansible supports what we call wildcards. We do this using the star (*) character. Wherever this wildcard appears, we are essentially instructing Ansible to substitute for any characters in the inventory hostname.

For example, we might target web-*:

```
ansible web-* --list-hosts
```

```
  hosts (2):
    web-001.local
    web-002
```

The text in **bold** is being matched against the wildcard in our host filter web-* (meaning web-*anything*). The wildcard character can appear anywhere in the host pattern – it doesn't necessarily need to be the end of the pattern. An example would be targeting web*.local:

```
ansible web*.local --list-hosts
```

```
  hosts (1):
    web-001.local
```

This time, because we specified .local at the end, we only matched on a single host because web-002 no longer matches the pattern. Conversely, we may put the wildcard at the start and match on all of a particular suffix such as *.local (or in reality *.mywebsite.com):

```
ansible *.local --list-hosts

  hosts (2):
    lb-001.local
    web-001.local
```

Regular Expressions and Host Ranges

Wildcards bring us nicely on to regular expressions. We will not deep dive here, as we could talk for hours about regular expressions, their power, and their pitfalls – but for our purposes, some simple basics are enough.

We can use some simple regular expression concepts to both **define** the hosts in our inventory file and to **filter** our hosts when running Ansible. First, let's take a look at defining hosts.

If we have many hosts with a similar naming convention, for example, we have ten web servers, all named web-001 to web-010. We can specify all such web servers on a single line in our inventory using a **range**.

Create a new file named ranges, and add the following:

```
[webservers]
web-0[01:10]
```

You can see we have used a new convention, two numbers between square brackets and separated by a colon. This is called a range and maps directly to [*start:end*]. In this case, we have defined ten hosts.

Let's run Ansible with *--list-hosts* to confirm:

```
> ansible webservers -i ranges --list-hosts
  hosts (10):
    web-001
    web-002
    web-003
    web-004
```

```
web-005
web-006
web-007
web-008
web-009
web-010
```

That saves a lot of typing when working with larger inventories of similar hosts, especially where there are no unique per-host variables.

We can also use regular expressions when **filtering** hosts on the Ansible command line. We generally do not do this, preferring to spend the time creating a good set of group names for our hosts. That is because the hosts that are targeted by regular expressions may change over time without you realizing – imagine you have web servers targeted using web* and you suddenly add a new host named website-storage-001, your regular expression will now erroneously include this new host. That cannot happen with well-designed Ansible groups.

Having said that, we will walk through a simple example as it is worth knowing the functionality exists. With a regular expression, we have some great power. For example, suppose we wanted to target both web-* and lb-*, but not db-* hosts. One might do so using the following regular expression:

```
ansible '~^(web|lb)*' --list-hosts
```

The tilde (~) at the start informs Ansible that what follows is a regular expression. Without this, ansible will attempt to take the input literally and will not find any matching hosts. What follows is a very simple regular expression; let's break it down:

```
^(web|lb)*
```

^ – This means "at the start of the hostname." For example, iweb-001 would not match since it does not start with web, but web-001 will.

(web|lb) – This means match anything where the word web or the word lb appears in this position, in this case, at the start of the hostname.

* – This is the wildcard, as we discussed previously, anything.

As you can see, regular expressions are a powerful way of filtering for hosts – but we rarely use them in practice. We much prefer well-thought-out groups and targeting based on those groups rather than having to craft complex and often changing filters every time we run Ansible.

Including and Excluding Hosts

All of our examples so far have focused on the hosts that we wish to include; conversely, we may want to **exclude** specific hosts from a group – for example, we want to target our load balancers, except for one specific host, which is down for maintenance. Or even we want to target all of our hosts, except for a small subset – an example might be making a change to all of your servers except the load balancers, because you want to avoid dropping user connections to the load balancer.

The key to excluding hosts and groups is the symbol representing logical NOT in computer science: this is most often represented as an exclamation mark (!).

Let's give it a go, using the **all** group, but then *excluding* the load_balancers group using the logical NOT (!) symbol:

```
> ansible 'all:!load_balancers' --list-hosts
  hosts (2):
    web-001.local
    web-002
```

We added single quotes around the host filter in the preceding command. That is because the Linux shell (bash) interprets the exclamation mark (!) as a special command. Adding single quotes instructs bash to not perform special processing on that part of the command.

You can start to see just how powerful this is – but the use cases for combining groups and not including others are not immediately obvious. You will use it when you start managing many thousands of production servers to perform staged rollouts or otherwise gather information from a subset of hosts.

A much more useful example for us would be the concept of a staging vs. production environment. A staging or preproduction environment is an often smaller-scale replica of our production service that can be used to deploy a recently developed version of code to gain confidence in its operation **before** putting it into our production environment.

Let's say we want to have web-001.local as our **production** web server, and we will use web-002 as our **staging** web server. They both have the same *function* as webservers, and so they both belong to the webservers group – but we need to further divide them by their *environment*.

It is important to understand that a single host in our Ansible inventory can belong to any number of groups. Once we have defined a host once in our Ansible inventory, we can refer to that host by only the inventory_ hostname from then on – meaning we do not need to specify the host variables each time we add the host to another group.

Let's take a look at what our staging and production groups would look like. Open the hosts inventory file, and add the new groups:

```
[webservers]
web-001.local
web-002 ansible_host=192.168.98.112

[load_balancers]
lb-001.local

[staging]
web-002

[production]
web-001.local
lb-001.local
```

Notice for web-002 we do **not** specify the host variables a second time. Ansible only needs the full host definition once, after which you can refer to that host using only the inventory_hostname. If you do specify any variables for a host a second time, those defined later in the inventory file will take precedence.

We can now target those new groups, staging and production, directly. But what if we want to target only the **production webservers**? Targeting the webservers group would include both the staging and production webservers, while targeting the production group would also include lb-001.local. This is where we use another special operator within our Ansible host filter – the logical **AND** represented by the ampersand symbol (&).

This tells Ansible to include all hosts that are a member of *both* group A AND group B only, meaning the host must exist in **both** groups to be included in our host list. In our case, we would filter on members of webservers that are also members of the production group.

Let's take a look at this in action:

```
> ansible 'webservers:&production' --list-hosts
  hosts (1):
    web-001.local
```

Beautiful. We are now able to independently target our staging webservers, our production webservers, our production load balancers, or even all of our staging or production environment. We could of course always still target **all** at any time.

Building your groups correctly brings you this power. We recommend splitting your inventory groups up according to both **function** and **environment** at the very least. Environment may relate to staging vs. production, as before, but could also relate to geographical region, for example. Later, we will talk about structuring your inventory for success, including using a directory of files as an inventory – adding even more flexibility to your group management.

Group the World: Groups of Groups

A group in the Ansible inventory need not only include hosts but can also contain other groups (known as a group of groups). This is often useful when splitting up your inventory into regional services; or you have a subset of your production servers running an upgraded package as part of a split test – where you want to determine if certain changes you have made either improve or degrade some important metric such as web page load time.

Imagine you have web servers spread across the world and require the flexibility to target your hosts by country or continent. Let's build such an inventory and take a look at groups of groups.

Create a new inventory file called `regional`:

```
[germany]
web-de-00[1:2]

[france]
web-fr-001

[netherlands]
web-nl-001

[spain]
web-es-00[1:3]

[usa]
web-us-00[1:4]
```

[europe:children]
```
germany
france
netherlands
spain
```

[americas:children]
```
usa
```

You may notice a new special convention in the group names highlighted in bold. Rather than just being a group name (as with Germany), they include a special addition **:children** – this instructs Ansible that the items included as group members are in fact other groups and not hosts, as would normally be the case. With this, Ansible will include all hosts that are members of the groups listed to become members of the new group.

Let's see how this looks by targeting one such group:

```
> ansible europe -i regional --list-hosts
  hosts (7):
    web-fr-001
    web-nl-001
    web-es-001
    web-es-002
    web-es-003
    web-de-001
    web-de-002
```

Wonderful. Ansible has listed all the hosts belonging to the groups named as members of the **europe** group. Now we have the power to target countries or regions.

This is super useful. Previously, we would have needed to add all of the hosts to multiple groups manually – there is a very high chance that over time the host lists diverge, for example, where a host is added to the "spain" group but is not missed from a "Europe" group. With groups of groups, that cannot happen – as soon as a host is added to spain, it is immediately a member of europe with no additional changes.

Combine this with environments such as staging/production, and you start to build an immensely powerful inventory that can be sliced and diced any way you see fit.

Setting Variables on the Group

We have covered slicing your groups by **function** (web servers, load balancers, database servers) and **environment** (staging vs. production, geographic regions). Now let's discuss another common logical grouping for Ansible – grouping by common attributes.

Often, this will follow your function group, for example, you may have an attribute of your web service which says all web servers run their HTTP service on port 8080. You could apply that directly to the webservers group. So we wish to set a variable called http_port to a value of 8080 for all webservers in the inventory.

Open up your original hosts inventory file once again, adding

```
[webservers]
web-001.local
web-002 ansible_host=192.168.98.112

[webservers:vars]
http_port=8080

[load_balancers]
lb-001.local

[staging]
web-002

[production]
web-001.local
lb-001.local
```

In bold, you'll find another special convention for the group name header **:vars** – this instructs ansible to apply the variables that follow to the host or group named before the colon, in this case *webservers*. We have created a variable in the form of key=value. This is an arbitrary variable name, meaning it has no intrinsic meaning to Ansible – but it will automatically be made available to any command we run via Ansible for these hosts.

To show you the impact this has, let's use a new Ansible module called *debug*:

```
> ansible all -m debug -a "var=http_port"
web-001.local | SUCCESS => {
    "http_port": 8080
}
web-002 | SUCCESS => {
    "http_port": 8080
}
lb-001.local | SUCCESS => {
    "http_port": "VARIABLE IS NOT DEFINED!"
}
```

The debug module is an informational module that is able to tell us information about specific variables or printing messages that we ask for from inside the Ansible execution. In this case, we asked it for information about a variable named http_port.

As you can see from the output, the variable we set in our inventory, http_port=8080, was available during the Ansible run for both of the hosts in the webservers group (web-001.local and web-002). The debug module further informed us that the other host lb-001.local, which was not part of the webservers group, does not have the variable named http_port defined – meaning the variable does not exist for that host.

Structuring Your Inventory for Success

You may be starting to realize that even with a very small inventory, our single file is already getting busy. We have hosts, groups, variables, and groups of groups all in a single file – and as our infrastructure grows, we will only add more hosts, more groups, and potentially more variables.

Think of this like a wardrobe. At first, you have a few tops and bottoms – you put them into an empty cupboard with no shelves or drawers. As time goes on, you start adding more clothes and do your best to keep them organized – but before long your socks are mixed with your underwear, your t-shirts and jumpers are jumbled in a pile, and you just can't find that pair of jeans you need without hunting through to the bottom of the pile. To make matters worse, you started sharing your wardrobe with your partner – who is just as disorganized!

What you really need is some structure. You need a wardrobe with some shelves, drawers, and hanging rails so that you can separate out all the different types of clothing. You have logically separated out your clothing into different spaces – this is more than just grouping them, this is grouping them **and** assigning them each their own location, allowing you to locate your t-shirts fast, grab some shorts, and throw together an outfit regardless of how many total items you now own.

The same is true of our inventory. So far, we have been adding groups and variables to our single file. We have arbitrarily decided to place these elements somewhere within the file that makes sense to us – but over time, the file will become unwieldy and difficult to navigate, especially when shared among a team of developers, just like in our initial disorganized wardrobe. We can organize our inventory better, and there are two complementary ways of achieving this; let's dive in.

Directory-Based Inventory

So far, we have had what is known as a file-based inventory, and we can specify that file (as we did for regional) every time we run Ansible with the -i regional option. But Ansible can be pointed at more than just a single file – we can tell Ansible to look at a directory instead.

When doing this, Ansible will parse **every** file inside the directory in alphabetical order and *try* to use it as part of its inventory. This means that we can split up our inventory across multiple files and put them all into a single directory.

Here's what we are going to do in the next few steps:

1. Create a new directory named inventory in our Ansible controller directory.

2. Move the webservers configuration from the current inventory file into a new file named webservers inside the new directory.

3. Move the load balancers configuration from the current inventory file into a new file named load_ balancers inside the new directory.

First, create the new directory named inventory/ – on the Linux command line, you would do this with

```
> mkdir inventory/
```

Next, create a new file named inventory/webservers:

```
[webservers]
web-001.local
web-002 ansible_host=192.168.98.112

[webservers:vars]
http_port=8080
```

Create a new file named inventory/load_balancers:

```
[load_balancers]
lb-001.local
```

Note   We will not migrate the staging/production groups to the new inventory, since they are not needed for this example. If we were to move them, we may have a third file named environments.

Now, let's point ansible at the new inventory/ directory and see if things still work the way we expect:

```
> ansible all -i inventory/ -m debug -a "var=http_port"
web-001.local | SUCCESS => {
    "http_port": 8080
}
web-002 | SUCCESS => {
    "http_port": 8080
}
lb-001.local | SUCCESS => {
    "http_port": "VARIABLE IS NOT DEFINED!"
}
```

All three of our hosts are there, and the http_port variable is set only on the webservers, exactly as expected. Now you can navigate your inventory with ease and always find what you are looking for.

To make life easier, you should modify your ansible.cfg file to point to the new inventory/ directory by default:

```
[defaults]
inventory = inventory/
```

Earlier, we mentioned that inventory files are included in alphabetical order. This is an important distinction – if you define the same host twice, the later definition will win. Great naming can really help here – define all of your host variables in their primary group (meaning for a web server, the web servers group) and then only include the hostname in any secondary groups (e.g., the production or staging group) to avoid confusion.

YAML Format Inventory

Even with separation of files based on function, INI format inventories can still quickly become unwieldy. This is like having your clothes all separated into shelves and drawers – but then not really folding them neatly within. Anything can be thrown anywhere in your underwear drawer, and over time – even though you know it only contains underwear – it will start to be difficult to find exactly what you want.

The same is true of Ansible INI format inventories. Variables, groups of groups, and hosts can be placed anywhere within the file. We are lacking **structure**. Ansible allows multiple formats for inventory files, INI being just one of them. We started with INI format, as it is the easiest to learn quickly and is the most common in use today – but we hope that will change moving forward for all the reasons we mentioned earlier.

Enter YAML format inventory files. There are several benefits to YAML for inventories:

1. YAML is what we will write most of our ansible code in; it is consistent. INI is not used anywhere else in Ansible.

2. YAML is structured; it won't become cluttered over time.

This is easiest to understand with an example. Let's take our inventory we created earlier and convert it to YAML.

Open the `inventory/webservers` file and replace the contents with this YAML format inventory:

```
---
webservers:
  hosts:
    web-001.local:
    web-002:
      ansible_host: 192.168.98.112
  vars:
    http_port: 8080
```

See what we mean by structured? No longer do we have a random header with a special tag to define variables which may not even be in the same file as the group itself – now everything is defined **beneath** the group name, using indented key-value pairs.

Most of this should be familiar: we have a group name (webservers), which contains hosts. There are two hosts, `web-001.local` and `web-002`, which have a host variable defining its IP address. We then have a **vars** section which is indented such that it belongs to the group – meaning the variable is assigned to all hosts within the group. This way, it is clear where all elements should live.

Go ahead and try it out:

```
ansible all -i inventory/ -m debug -a "var=http_port"

web-001.local | SUCCESS => {
    "http_port": 8080
}
web-002 | SUCCESS => {
    "http_port": 8080
}
```

```
lb-001.local | SUCCESS => {
    "http_port": "VARIABLE IS NOT DEFINED!"
}
```

What's interesting here is that we still see our lb-001.local host. That is still defined in the old INI format inventory file. Ansible allows you to mix and match – it parses every file in the inventory directory and determines which format to use on a file by file basis.

Following on with the YAML format inventory, to create our regional groups of groups, this is how it would now look:

```
---
germany:
  hosts:
    web-de-00[1:2]:
france:
  hosts:
    web-fr-001:
spain:
  hosts:
    web-es-00[1:3]:
usa:
  hosts:
    web-us-00[1:4]:

europe:
  children:
    germany:
    france:
    spain:
americas:
  children:
    usa:
```

For any new inventory file, we would strongly recommend this YAML format. We introduced the INI format first as it is simply easier to build up and understand the concepts. Now you have a good grasp on how inventories work – try migrating the load balancer inventory to YAML by yourself, using the `--list-hosts` command to verify.

Summary

We have covered a great deal in this chapter, and by now you are probably an Ansible inventory expert (and also sick of hearing the word inventory). We really can't stress enough how important it is to become familiar with these concepts – the ability to inventory is your ability to keep your Ansible commands simple and avoid making costly mistakes.

We have covered simple inventories, defined hosts, and then added them to groups to make our life easier. We have explored how to set variables on a single host and on a group of hosts to ensure we can both connect to the right servers and set our own configuration variables. We looked at the power of Ansible host filters combining multiple hostnames and groups, selecting only those hosts that belong to multiple groups and even including a larger grouping and excluding specific hosts or groups from it. These are all powerful skills to have on the Ansible command line and will prevent you having to constantly modify source code files later.

We then took it a step further – looking at how groups can become members of other groups to create structure, such as cities, countries, regions, and the world. This can be applied in any number of ways to enhance the ability to manage your servers.

Finally, we wrapped up the chapter discussing how to structure your inventory for success – splitting it up into logically ordered files and embracing the newer YAML format inventory file for improved structure and easier maintenance moving forward. I feel my Aunt would be happy to get into that car and drive to the destination now we can give her such detailed instructions.

CHAPTER 4

Your First Playbook

It is assumed at this stage that you have followed along with the exercises in the previous chapters and therefore have a working

1. Vagrant environment up and running

2. Inventory file with correct groups

3. Ansible configuration file

If that is not the case, please download the source code accompanying this book and copy the files from the Chapter 3 directory.

Modules and Tasks

In the previous chapters, we introduced you to the concept of a *module*, and we made use of a module called *shell* to run specific commands such as *hostname* on our target host. The *shell* module is an example of one that is built into Ansible – there are many such modules, and we will use a variety throughout our journey. Chapter 5 will deep dive into modules.

Typically, we used the *shell* module by using the ansible ad hoc command and passing the *-m* to specify which module to run, along with *-a* to specify any attributes to pass into the module. We could just as easily use any other Ansible module with our ad hoc command. Take, for example, the hostname module; the ad hoc command to set the hostname would look like this:

```
> ansible web-001 -m hostname -a name=web-001
```

© Shaun R Smith and Peter Membrey 2022
S. R. Smith and P. Membrey, *Beginning Ansible Concepts and Application*,
https://doi.org/10.1007/978-1-4842-8173-4_4

That is all well and good, but it is a single module, a single "task." It doesn't allow us to orchestrate the state of all our services, configurations, and content as promised. For that, we need something called playbooks, and Ansible playbooks at their core are a collection of these *tasks*.

The way we express that we want to execute a module with a specific set of attributes within an Ansible playbook is through a *task* definition. Tasks are an invocation of a module, executed against one or more target hosts, to perform some action. A task might use a module to affect a change by

1. Running shell commands directly on the host

2. Installing an application

3. Modifying a system configuration file

4. Uploading a new configuration file

5. Syncing content for a website

6. Restarting a service

One task does one thing. It may do that one thing multiple times, in the case of targeting multiple hosts or even using a loop – something we'll get into later. But for now, one task is responsible for one action, one change, to the target host.

This is best shown with an example task:

```
- name: Set the hostname
  hostname:
    name: my-webserver
```

This task has

1. A name that is shown when the playbook is run
   using Ansible

2. A module – In this case, the module called hostname

3. Attributes – In this case, a variable called name with
    the value my-webserver

The result of executing this task would be that the module called
hostname sets the hostname of the target host to my-webserver.

Let's try this out; we can run the preceding task in a *playbook* (as
shown earlier), which we will cover shortly, or with our familiar ansible ad
hoc command:

```
ansible web-001.local -m hostname -a name=web-001

web-001.local | SUCCESS => {
    "ansible_facts": {
        "ansible_domain": "",
        "ansible_fqdn": "web-001",
        "ansible_hostname": "web-001",
        "ansible_nodename": "web-001",
        "discovered_interpreter_python": "/usr/bin/python3"
    },
    "changed": false,
    "name": "web-001"
}
```

This ad hoc command closely resembles the "task" defined earlier.
We specify the *module* to use: hostname using the -m flag and then the
attributes to pass to the module using the -a flag. These attributes match
those we defined for the task name=my-webserver. The purpose of this
example is to show you that a module and its attributes are no different
under the hood whether you use an ad hoc command or a playbook task.

At the very core, a single "task" in an Ansible playbook executes one
single *module* with attributes that you control. Think of a task as you
running a program on your computer: you know the name of the program

(say, *ssh*) and you know the attributes it needs, such as the hostname of the server that you wish to connect to. You trust that every time you run that program, with those attributes, it will take the same action – it is well tested and repeatable.

In this case, *ssh* would be the *module* and the *hostname* the parameter.

Structuring Your Tasks: Playbooks

Playbooks are the real power behind Ansible. Playbooks allow you to group an infinite number of "tasks" to be executed against one, many, or all of the servers defined in your inventory – be it grouped by function, such as web servers vs. email servers, or by environment such as staging vs. production. Think of a playbook in its simplest form as the *glue* between three core components:

1. Inventory – The managed hosts you wish to target

2. Configuration – Things like the `http_port` configuration item

3. Tasks – The modules you wish to execute against those hosts

Inside the playbook at the highest level, we define a "play." The play is simply a grouping of hosts to a set of tasks. Allowing a playbook to have multiple plays enables Ansible to manage multi-machine and multi-environment deployments. Imagine you have multiple web servers that need upgrading, with a load balancer – your "plays" to upgrade each web server might look something like

1. LB – Remove one backend web server from the pool

2. WEB – Upgrade the web server's nginx to the latest release

3. WEB – Restart the backend web servers

4. WEB – Test that the upgraded web server is responding

5. LB – Add the web server back into the load balancer pool

6. REPEAT until each web server is upgraded

All of this can be achieved using a single playbook (meaning a **single** ansible command), with multiple plays orchestrating the different tasks against different hosts in a specific order. Therefore, you might jump back and forth between different host groups; you might stop on failure or be willing to accept a 10% failure rate. This playbook design allows for any normal manual process to be defined in code.

Playbooks are incredibly powerful. They are the core of Ansible. You can leverage a great deal of power from Ansible while only understanding playbooks. Other features such as roles, which we will discuss later, are there primarily to help you organize and reuse your playbooks as they grow.

Building Up Your Playbook

Let's get started with the basics of our playbook. You should write this out yourself to get familiar with the structure and formatting. Note that indentation is **necessary**; it is part of YAML much like with Python.

Many text editors can understand and therefore help with YAML formatting, either natively or through a plugin. To get started, we recommend Sublime Text as it is available on most platforms.

Create a file in your work area called `webservers.yml`:

```
---
- hosts: webservers
  tasks:
    - name: Ensure nginx is installed
      apt:
        name: nginx
        state: present
```

Let us work through that step by step:

```
- hosts: webservers
```

This is the start of a "play" – defining the hosts that you are targeting. This follows the host pattern rules discussed in the previous chapter – it can include individual hostnames, ranges, group names as defined in your Ansible inventory file, or any combination of them. In this case, we are targeting the `webservers` group that we created in our inventory file.

```
  tasks:
```

Tell Ansible that what follows are the *tasks* that we want to execute as a part of this play. There are other keywords that we might use here which will help us stay organized as our playbook grows larger, but for now we'll simply define the *tasks*.

```
    - name: Ensure nginx is installed
      apt:
        name: nginx
        state: present
```

The structure of the task should be familiar from when we set the hostname previously. Here, we are naming the task and then telling Ansible to use the built-in module apt, which is a package manager – responsible for installing/removing packages on Debian/Ubuntu-based operating systems.

We are then passing in the parameters. In this case

1. name – The name of the package that we wish to affect.

2. state – The state we want that package to be in, in this case present, meaning installed. Remember we are declaring the desired state, not telling Ansible how to get there.

Note   This *could* also be defined as an ad hoc command with

```
ansible -m apt -a "name=nginx state=present" host
```

Execute the Playbook

Let's run our playbook against our two web servers. This time, rather than using the ansible command, for running ad hoc tasks against a host, we will use the ansible-playbook command:

```
> ansible-playbook webservers.yml

PLAY [webservers] ****************************************
**********

TASK [Gathering Facts] **********************************
*************
ok: [web-001.local]

TASK [Ensure nginx is installed] ************************
**********************
fatal: [web-001.local]: FAILED! => {"changed": false, "cmd":
"apt-get update", "msg": "E: Could not open lock file /var/lib/
apt/lists/lock - open (13: Permission denied)\nE: Unable to
lock directory /var/lib/apt/lists/\n
```

```
<truncated>

        to retry, use: --limit @/vagrant/ansible/webservers.
        yml.retry

PLAY RECAP ******************************************************
web-001.local               :
ok=1     changed=0     unreachable=0     failed=1
```

Oh no! We got a very ugly-looking error message! It really isn't obvious at this point what is going wrong – unfortunately, Ansible isn't great at interpreting errors and providing human-readable output for many modules.

In this case, looking through the error output we should see a lot of mentions about **permission denied** as highlighted earlier. That is because we are connecting to the web-001 and web-002 hosts without specifying a username with admin (root) access. In Ubuntu, only users with administrative permissions are able to manage package installation, and as such we get this permission denied message when Ansible needs to make a change to a package's state.

Power user hint: You can make output much more readable by setting a configuration option for output format to debug by adding the following to the [defaults] section in your ansible.cfg file:

```
stdout_callback = debug
```

Becoming the All-Powerful Root User

This problem will affect most commands we will run via Ansible playbooks; therefore, we will need to *become* the root user when connecting via Ansible.

This is achieved using an Ansible keyword: become – meaning to escalate your privilege from the current connecting user to an administrator. There are many ways of doing this, but for now let's assume the most common (and also Ansible's default): *sudo*.

Luckily for us, we don't need to tell Ansible to use sudo. We simply declare that we would like to become a different user. We can do this at various levels:

1.   Globally in the ansible configuration file.

2.   Per host or group (including the *all* group) in our inventory file.

3.   For the entire playbook, regardless of the hosts we target.

4.   At the task level, where we control which tasks are read-only vs. write. In practice, this isn't useful in most cases.

For our purposes, let's add *become* to our playbook. We like to do this as it is explicit – meaning reading the playbook makes it very clear that we depend on administrative access. When set globally or via the hosts in the inventory, it is more likely we will take this behavior for granted or forget it exists in the future.

Modify the playbook `webservers.yml`:

```
---
- hosts: webservers
  become: true
  tasks:
    - name: Ensure nginx is installed
      apt:
        name: nginx
        state: present
```

Now run the playbook again, this time hopefully without an error:

```
> ansible-playbook webservers.yml
```

After a slight pause, you should see some interesting output – this is where you start to realize the true power of Ansible.

```
PLAY [webservers] ****

TASK [Gathering Facts] ****
ok: [web-001]
ok: [web-002]

TASK [Ensure nginx is installed] ****
changed: [web-002]
changed: [web-001]

PLAY RECAP ****
web-001   : ok=2 changed=1 unreachable=0 failed=0
web-002   : ok=2 changed=1 unreachable=0 failed=0
```

We executed a "play" called webservers. This is named after the hosts that we targeted in our playbook. Remember, there can be multiple plays in a playbook – always targeting specific groups of hosts.

```
TASK [Gathering Facts] ****
ok: [web-001]
ok: [web-002]

TASK [Ensure nginx is installed] ****
changed: [web-002]
changed: [web-001]
```

We see two tasks. Odd, we only specified one task in our playbook.

The first task, as mentioned earlier, is executing the setup module. Ansible names this task *Gathering Facts* – and it will run automatically at the start of *every* play you define. The values of those facts are imported into your playbook and can be used as variables, as we'll see later.

The second task is our installation of nginx. Notice that the output shows each of the two target hosts in the webservers group on a separate line, along with a status changed. This status will always be one of

- ok – No modification was necessary on the target host.

- changed – The configuration on the host was modified.

- unreachable – The host could not be contacted.

- failed – An error occurred while attempting to make the change.

```
PLAY RECAP ****
web-001  : ok=2 changed=1 unreachable=0 failed=0
web-002  : ok=2 changed=1 unreachable=0 failed=0
```

We are then presented with a Play Recap – listing each host that the play targeted along with the number of each task status encountered for each host.

Check the Results

To confirm nginx was installed as expected, open up a web browser on your computer and go to the URL of one of the web servers: http://192.168.98.111/.

You should see the "Welcome to nginx" page.

Congratulations – you have just executed your first Ansible playbook!

Pushing Files

Obviously, installing nginx is not all that useful by itself. We could have done that using an ad hoc command from the previous chapter – so let's get more creative and actually push our own home page to the server.

First, let's create a very simple home page. Create a directory named files in your work directory, and inside that create a new file named index.html with the following content:

```
This is my website which was setup using Ansible
```

Going back to the webservers.yml playbook, add a new task which will push this index.html file to the web server host(s):

```
---
- hosts: webservers
  become: true
  tasks:
    - name: Ensure nginx is installed
      apt:
        name: nginx
        state: present

- name: Push website content to the web root
  copy:
    src: index.html
    dest: /var/www/html/
    mode: u=rw,g=r,o=r
```

Here, we are using the copy module to push a file from the local directory to the remove host. Note: We do not specify the files directory that we created as part of the src. That's because the copy module will automatically look for files inside the files directory. We always specify the mode (permissions) that the resulting file should have – it is important, but not required by Ansible, for this to be explicit. Doing so prevents mistakes such as accidentally exposing content you didn't mean to be public or introducing a security risk to your environment. It also makes security auditing simpler when needed.

Execute the Playbook

```
> ansible-playbook webservers.yml

PLAY [webservers] ****

TASK [Gathering Facts] ****
ok: [web-002]
ok: [web-001]

TASK [Ensure nginx is installed] ****
ok: [web-002]
ok: [web-001]

TASK [Push website content to the web root] ****
changed: [web-002]
changed: [web-001]

PLAY RECAP ****
web-001    : ok=3 changed=1 unreachable=0 failed=0
web-002    : ok=3 changed=1 unreachable=0 failed=0
```

Now, with a successful run, our content should be served by the web server we have set up. Check the content for the web page on webserver web-001 by visiting or refreshing the page at http://192.168.98.111/.

You should now see your custom home page. The same should be true for web-002 also at http://192.168.98.112/.

A Note on Idempotence

You will notice something particularly important in the output of this second playbook run. Rather than **changed**, as it was previously, the status for the nginx install task now shows as **ok** – meaning no change was needed.

81

This is what we mean when we say Ansible is "idempotent." When we declare a task, we are defining the state that we desire that module to get the host to. All modules are designed to be idempotent, meaning if no action is needed, then nothing will be changed. We will see the true power of this later, where we will be restarting a service on configuration file change – wouldn't it be terrible if the configuration file **always** changed? Our users would not be happy with the service constantly going down.

Try for yourself by running the exact same playbook a second time, with no changes made to your code:

```
> ansible-playbook webservers.yml

PLAY [webservers] ****

TASK [Gathering Facts] ****
ok: [web-002]
ok: [web-001]

TASK [Ensure nginx is installed] ****
ok: [web-002]
ok: [web-001]

TASK [Push website content to the web root] ****
ok: [web-001]
ok: [web-002]

PLAY RECAP ****
web-001  : ok=3 changed=0 unreachable=0 failed=0
web-002  : ok=3 changed=0 unreachable=0 failed=0
```

Notice this time there were **no changes** to the target servers. That's because there was nothing to change. The index.html file on the server is identical to the one we are trying to push – in that case, Ansible will do nothing.

Now, change the content in files/index.html to read

```
Welcome to my Ansible-provisioned website!
```

Then run your playbook once again, noting that no other changes have been made to tell Ansible to do anything different:

```
> ansible-playbook webservers.yml

PLAY [webservers] ****

TASK [Gathering Facts] ****
ok: [web-002]
ok: [web-001]

TASK [Ensure nginx is installed] ****
ok: [web-002]
ok: [web-001]

TASK [Push website content to the web root] ****
changed: [web-002]
changed: [web-001]

PLAY RECAP ****
web-001: ok=3 changed=1 unreachable=0 failed=0
web-002: ok=3 changed=1 unreachable=0 failed=0
```

Great! Ansible realized that the index.html file that was already on the host was **different** to the local index.html file and updated it for us.

Syntax Checking Your Playbooks

The authors are big proponents of testing early and often. There are always many ways to improve your code quality, but one simple thing we can do early on is to syntax check our ansible playbooks. Think of this as the equivalent of testing the configuration file syntax for nginx. It confirms that you have not made any simple syntax mistakes that might prevent your playbook from running.

To do this for our preceding playbook, simply run

```
> ansible-playbook webservers.yml --syntax-check

playbook: webservers.yml
```

This output shows no errors; the syntax is good.

Let's introduce a mistake. Open webservers.yml, and add a task with invalid formatting (in this case, bad indentation for the hostname):

```
- name: this is a broken task
  hostname:
name: bad-indentation
```

Now, run the syntax check again:

```
> ansible-playbook webservers.yml --syntax-check

ERROR! Syntax Error while loading YAML.
  did not find expected '-' indicator

The error appears to have been in '/vagrant/ansible/webservers.
yml': line 18, column 5, but may be elsewhere in the file
depending on the exact syntax problem.

The offending line appears to be:

      hostname:
    invalid: parameter
    ^ here
```

The error message is not super obvious, due to the many things that could have gone wrong with this input. But it does show you the offending line and point out that your playbook has an error.

Now, try to run the playbook without a syntax check:

```
ansible-playbook webservers.yml
```

```
ERROR! Syntax Error while loading YAML.
  did not find expected '-' indicator
```

The error appears to have been in '/vagrant/ansible/webservers.yml': line 18, column 5, but may be elsewhere in the file depending on the exact syntax problem.

The offending line appears to be:

```
    hostname:
  invalid: parameter
^ here
```

The same error. `ansible-playbook` is automatically syntax checking our playbook before executing it. That is very handy.

Don't forget to remove this broken task from your playbook; otherwise, you will be debugging a syntax error on your next journey!

Then why run `syntax-check` manually? Manual syntax checks can be a great way to catch errors early – especially in situations where you don't necessarily want to run the playbook against target hosts or may not have access to secrets such as SSH keys. Imagine you want to include these checks as part of a test suite in a continuous integration system or have it validated before performing a `git` push to prevent broken code from reaching your Git repository.

Summary

Ansible has playbooks, playbooks contain plays, and plays contain tasks. Tasks are simply a means of invoking a module with attributes.

That is the core structure of Ansible. Everything else is some combination or extension of these building blocks designed to help you structure, secure, and control the flow of tasks within your plays in creative ways to effectively achieve the automation of any process.

As you build up your foundation knowledge, you will start looking at complex playbooks and seeing the simplicity that comes from sticking to declarative and idempotent tasks. You will begin to see this structure repeated with added flare.

In this chapter, you wrote your first Ansible playbook and experienced just how few lines of code are needed to produce a functioning web server with some basic content. You ran that playbook against multiple servers – creating two identical copies of your new web server. It is worth considering that whether you are working with 1 web server or 100 web servers, the code you wrote doesn't change. As a reference, our team currently deploys >3000 production servers with confidence, using the same Ansible playbooks that were written for 10 servers during development.

We then explored idempotence in a practical way – an especially important topic. This allows you to rerun the same playbook against the same host multiple times – if no change is needed, no change is made.

Finally, we introduced one of Ansible's safety nets, syntax checking. This happens before any code is executed whether you ask for it or not. There are many other (and better) ways of testing your playbooks – which we will cover more of in later chapters. But at least you know you will always get feedback if you make any syntactical errors in your playbooks.

CHAPTER 5

Batteries Included: Ansible Modules

In previous chapters, we have already used a few simple modules, namely, hostname to set the server's hostname, apt to install nginx, shell to execute arbitrary commands, and copy to push configuration files to the server. We have looked at how we call a module and pass in arguments which tell the module what we hope to achieve.

We will now deep dive into Ansible modules to show how those simple concepts can be turned into a powerful force – by using a variety of arguments, a single module can achieve many results. We can interpret those results in many ways, and some results will even affect the success/failure of your overall playbook.

We have used modules in two distinct ways, via the ansible ad hoc command and via a task in a playbook. The ad hoc command is great for running a single module against a set of hosts, but it does not provide repeatability; therefore, we will now focus on defining our modules as tasks in a playbook – since that is likely to account for the majority of our Ansible use.

There are many modules included in Ansible out of the box, with some common ones listed in Table 5-1, each designed to do one thing and do it well. They vary a lot. They are written by various people and teams. You can write your own. They can be written in any language (although often

© Shaun R Smith and Peter Membrey 2022
S. R. Smith and P. Membrey, *Beginning Ansible Concepts and Application*,
https://doi.org/10.1007/978-1-4842-8173-4_5

Python is the language of choice). They can achieve anything you could imagine doing against a host – be it a Linux server or network switch. There are however several features that all ansible modules have in common:

1.   Their arguments should be declarative.

2.   Their actions should be idempotent.

3.   Their output will always be consistent and understood by Ansible.

With those three attributes, a module can be and do anything.

Table 5-1 describes a few important modules that might be used throughout our Ansible journey, giving you some idea as to the breadth of modules available.

Table 5-1. *Common Ansible Modules*

Module	Description
Apt/yum	Instruct the package manager to install, uninstall, or upgrade packages
Copy	Copy a file from the Ansible controller to the remote host
Fetch	Copy a file from the remote host to the Ansible controller
File	Create or delete files, directories, and links; change ownership and permissions
Git	Manage git repository clones, pull changes, check out branches
Iptables/ufw	Manage firewall rules on Linux servers that support iptables or ufw
Reboot	Reboot the remote host, with timeouts and custom messages
Service/ systemd	Start, stop, restart, enable, and disable services via most Linux service managers
User	Manage user accounts on remote Linux hosts
Wait_for	Wait_for something to happen before continuing executing the playbook, such as timeouts or a file being present

Where Do Modules Come From?

As Ansible is an open source project, with a very active community, many modules are developed by different groups of people. Some are Ansible core modules, meaning they are written by the Ansible engineering team themselves and are often guaranteed to remain backward compatible into the future. Others, such as hostname, are community modules, meaning they are created and maintained by the Ansible community. This distinction became important as Ansible grew drastically in size and was taken under the Red Hat umbrella that offer various support services atop Ansible.

For the most part, you may not need to worry about this distinction, but there are some cases that it may become important in the future. If you are working in an environment requiring strong security compliance or have taken out a support contract for Ansible with Red Hat, then you are more likely to stick to core and certified modules. If things go wrong with a community module, then you are much less likely to get fast responses to your concerns, relying on very smart individuals whose primary job is not Ansible, doing the best they can to help.

Exploring the *apt* Module

Let's focus on a single module and see how we can bend it to our will using the arguments that we pass to it. We will explore various ways of using the module, along with its output and how Ansible understands what is going on to provide you a simple status update.

Before we get started, we will need to modify our Ansible configuration file. That is because the more detailed output from Ansible, while useful, defaults to a format that can be somewhat difficult to read. Therefore, we shall first set a configuration option in the ansible.cfg file to help format this output better.

Open or create the file `ansible.cfg`, and ensure the content looks like the following. The addition is highlighted in bold:

```
[defaults]
inventory = inventory
stdout_callback = yaml
```

This new line tells ansible to use a yaml plugin for printing lines to the screen, which is also known as standard out, or stdout.

Next, we will create our playbook in a new file named `exploring-apt.yml` and add the following simple task:

```
---
- hosts: web-001.local
  become: true
  tasks:
    - name: Ensure nginx is installed
      apt:
        name: nginx
        state: present

    - name: Uninstall tree command
      apt:
        name: tree
        state: absent
```

The first task "Ensure nginx is installed" is identical to the one we used in the previous chapter. This is declaring that the end state of running this task should be that the apt package named *nginx* is *present* or installed.

The second task however is new. Here, we have replaced the state *present* for the word *absent*. Remember we are being declarative, and the module is idempotent – meaning Ansible will only make changes *if* they are required to bring the host into this state. The module is responsible for figuring out the *how*.

We are asking the apt module to ensure the application named tree is **not** installed.

The tree is a simple application which lists directory contents in a structured tree format. It is quite useful, but we don't need it for our web servers, so it is safe to remove.

Let's run this playbook, using a new flag to ansible-playbook called *verbose* or -*v*, telling it to provide more detailed output. This output will be structured using yaml, thanks to the configuration change we made at the start of this chapter.

```
> ansible-playbook exploring-apt.yml -v

PLAY [web-001.local] ****

TASK [Gathering Facts] ****
ok: [web-001.local]

TASK [Ensure nginx is installed] ****
ok: [web-001.local] => changed=false
  cache_update_time: 1596011857
  cache_updated: false

TASK [Uninstall tree command] ****
changed: [web-001.local] => changed=true
  stderr: ''
  stderr_lines: []
  stdout: |-
    Reading package lists...
```

```
   Building dependency tree...
   Reading state information...
   The following packages will be REMOVED:
     tree
   0 upgraded, 0 newly installed, 1 to remove and 51 not
   upgraded.
   Remv tree [1.7.0-5]
  stdout_lines: <omitted>
PLAY RECAP ****
web-001.local  : ok=3 changed=1 unreachable=0 failed=0
```

If your output shows a different status for the tasks, it could be that you have run tasks out of order or rebuilt your vagrant environment. That is nothing to worry about – ansible is doing its job and achieving your desired state.

Let's walk through the output from these two tasks. First, we will take a look at the repeat task for installing nginx which now includes more information than it did previously thanks to the *verbose* option.

```
TASK [Ensure nginx is installed] ****
ok: [web-001.local] => changed=false
  cache_update_time: 1596011857
  cache_updated: false
```

Here, we are shown the status of the task, along with the hostname as usual. However, there is additional information in the form of key=value pairs such as changed=false. These values are being sent back to Ansible from the module itself and are either providing information directly to Ansible or debugging information to help us figure out what is happening under the hood.

Ansible has determined the status for this task to be "ok," meaning no changes were needed. It has derived that from the field named changed from the module, which has a value of false.

Variables that can have one of two values, yes or no, are known as Boolean. A "yes" is represented by Boolean True, and "no" is represented by Boolean False. In Ansible, Boolean values are case insensitive, and you can use yes/no/true/false.

Following these are two more key-value pairs, describing the state of a *cache*. This is a uniquely apt concept, referring to a cache of all of the packages currently available to install. You would often update this cache before installing a package using apt update, to ensure you are getting the latest versions available. The apt module in ansible is also able to manage the cache and reports back to us what its state is while running this task.

In this case, cache_updated is set to false, meaning the module did **not** update the apt cache while running this task. It also reports the cache_update_time, meaning the time at which the cache was last updated, as a unix timestamp.

Why should you care? Well, as outlined earlier, before installing a package you would often want to update the cache. However, that isn't a very idempotent action – since updating the cache every time you use the apt module would be changing something repeatedly on the remote host. To achieve this, the apt module allows us to only refresh the cache when a certain period of time has passed since the last update. We will do this shortly – but first let us dive into the second task's output:

```
TASK [Uninstall tree command] ****
changed: [web-001.local] => changed=true
  stderr: ''
  stderr_lines: []
```

```
stdout: |-
  Reading package lists...
  Building dependency tree...
  Reading state information...
  The following packages will be REMOVED:
    tree
  0 upgraded, 0 newly installed, 1 to remove and 51 not
  upgraded.
  Remv tree [1.7.0-5]
stdout_lines: <omitted>
```

This task is different. Ansible reports the status as "changed" rather than "ok," meaning it made a change to the remote host. It derived this from the value of changed being true (or yes).

Ansible then presents some additional key-value pairs that we have not seen before: stderr, stderr_lines, stdout, and stdout_lines. These refer directly to the output of running the module on the remote host – those variables with the suffix _lines are simply the same content as those without but are split into a programmatic list for easier parsing (just like using the str.split() function in Python).

stderr, or standard error, reports output that was sent as part of an error message. In this case, it is empty, since there were no errors reported. stdout or standard output reports the normal output from the module just as you would have seen it had you run apt uninstall tree on the command line.

The module can send back any relevant information. Ansible only depends directly on a couple of critical pieces of information:

1. Was there an error? If the key-value is returned, assume not.

2. Was something changed?

Everything else is there for either debugging or to help you in controlling the flow of your ansible playbooks, something we'll cover more later.

Updating the apt Cache

As mentioned earlier, we can instruct the ansible module to update the apt cache if needed. To do this, we need to tell the module what an appropriate age for the cache is – or put another way, how old can the cache be without needing to update it.

For now, we can use something short, to ensure an update happens on our next Ansible run. Note we only care about the cache being up to date when installing packages, not removing them. That is because the cache determines the version of a package that will be installed and where to get it from – information that changes frequently.

```
---
- hosts: web-001.local
  become: true
  tasks:
    - name: Ensure nginx is installed
      apt:
        name: nginx
        state: present
        cache_valid_time: 60

    - name: Uninstall tree command
      apt:
        name: tree
        state: absent
```

The cache_valid_time argument takes a value in seconds, meaning the allowed age of the cache in number of seconds. Run that playbook again, remembering the *verbose* flag:

```
> ansible-playbook exploring-apt.yml -v

PLAY [web-001.local] ****

TASK [Gathering Facts] ****
ok: [web-001.local]

TASK [Ensure nginx is installed] ****
ok: [web-001.local] => changed=false
  cache_update_time: 1596015102
  cache_updated: true

TASK [Uninstall tree command] ****
ok: [web-001.local] => changed=false

PLAY RECAP ****
web-001.local   : ok=3 changed=0 unreachable=0 failed=0
```

Notice that the task we set cache_valid_time on now reports the value for cache_updated as true (or yes). That's because the time since the previous update was greater than 60 seconds ago. If you'd like to see this in action, run the same playbook twice within 60 seconds (or set a longer cache_valid_time) and observe the output vary depending on whether that time has expired or not.

This is how we build on the basics – gaining more control and more flexibility in the way the module operates due to the arguments we pass in and our understanding of the output we get back.

Upgrading Packages

In keeping with the theme of package management, the apt module can not only install and remove packages, it can also upgrade those that are already installed. Being declarative, we don't tell Ansible how to perform the upgrade – just that we expect the package to be in an upgraded state.

To ensure a single package is always up to date, we *can* tell the apt module that we expect the package to be the latest available. Take, for example, the following task:

```
- name: Ensure nginx is installed
  apt:
    name: nginx
    state: latest
    cache_valid_time: 60
```

Upon running this, nginx would be upgraded *only if* the version installed is not the current latest version. If it is not the latest version when the playbook is next run, it will be upgraded.

On the surface, this can seem like a great idea, but a word of caution – this action damages the idempotence that is so critical to our production environments. Suddenly, the *same* playbook being run against the *same* server will not leave that server in the same state the second time should the package have an update available, as it will automatically upgrade it.

Understanding how apt works is also crucial here: when upgrading a package via apt, the service that has been upgraded is **automatically restarted**, meaning our well-intentioned playbook to ensure nginx on the web servers is always up to date just resulted in production downtime.

If you'd like to explore this concept, we have included an optional exercise at the end of this Chapter.

Upgrading All Packages

Suppose you really do want to perform an upgrade of your packages. This should be a selective and conscious action and therefore performed in a separate playbook, rather than using latest as a state in your production playbooks.

Alternatively, to achieve upgrades of all packages on the remote host, the apt module provides an upgrade argument. Let's create an upgrade playbook that we can point at any of our remote hosts to perform a full package upgrade. Create a new file upgrade.yml:

```
---
- hosts: web-001.local
  become: true
  tasks:
    - name: Upgrade all packages
      apt:
        upgrade: dist
        update_cache: yes
```

This task is telling the apt module that it should always update the cache before taking any action (after all, an upgrade requires the latest packages). It then tells the module to perform a dist upgrade, meaning upgrade all packages on the host including the core operating system such as the kernel.

Running this playbook will result in a full upgrade of the remote host, and any services that have been upgraded will be automatically restarted. Remember, that may mean production outages:

```
> ansible-playbook upgrade.yml -v

PLAY [web-001.local] ****

TASK [Gathering Facts] ****
ok: [web-001.local]
```

```
TASK [Upgrade all packages] ****
changed: [web-001.local] => changed=true
  msg: |-
    Reading package lists...
    Building dependency tree...
    Reading state information...
    Calculating upgrade...

    <truncate lots of output>

PLAY RECAP ****
web-001.local : ok=2 changed=1 unreachable=0 failed=0
```

Using the verbose flag, Ansible presents the full output from the upgrade which will likely include a lot of package names and status updates. After this playbook has run, the remote host's packages will be totally up to date; however, a system restart is likely required to fully apply some of those updates. Thankfully, there is a module for that.

```
---
- hosts: web-001.local
  become: true
  tasks:
    - name: Upgrade all packages
      apt:
        upgrade: dist
        update_cache: yes
- name: Reboot the host
  reboot:
```

This introduced a new module – the deceptively simple reboot module, with no arguments, will cause the host to immediately reboot (no surprises there), then wait for it to come back up before allowing the playbook to continue.

Learning Modules

It should start becoming clear that the apt module is extremely powerful. It can install, uninstall, and upgrade packages; manage the apt cache; automatically remove packages that are no longer needed; and a whole host of other features. That is just a *single* module, of which there are hundreds.

With new features and new modules coming into existence all the time, Ansible is an exciting and constantly evolving application. Clearly, we need a reliable way of learning how to use each module.

To understand the attributes available to your module, you can use the ansible-doc command, as introduced in Chapter 2:

```
> ansible-doc apt
```

This document is split into multiple sections, including one describing each of the elements we walked through for apt:

1. Options or arguments that can be passed into the module

2. Examples of various uses of the module

3. Return values that are seen via ansible-playbook tasks using the verbose flag

---

It is often easier to read and understand a module using the online documentation by typing the module name into the search box at the top of this website: https://docs.ansible.com/ansible/.

Exploring More Modules

Up to now, we have a web server running with some custom content via the webservers.yml playbook, and that server is completely up to date thanks to the upgrade.yml playbook. But it doesn't really *do* much, does it?

Now we will modify our webservers.yml playbook and add a selection of new tasks. The goal here is to explore a few new modules and become familiar with their format while

1. Installing nginx

2. Managing some content using various modules

3. Setting up a basic firewall

```
---
- hosts: webservers
  become: true
  tasks:
    - name: Ensure nginx is installed
      apt:
        name: nginx
        state: present

    - name: Push website content to the web root
      copy:
        src: index.html
        dest: /var/www/html/
        mode: u=rw,g=r,o=r

    - name: index.html also known as main.html
      file:
        state: link
        src: /var/www/html/index.html
        dest: /var/www/html/main.html
```

```
- name: Update the website content
  lineinfile:
    path: /var/www/html/index.html
    line: "Just re-decorating a little!"

- name: Firewall - Allow SSH connections
  ufw:
    rule: allow
    name: OpenSSH

- name: Firewall - Allow website connections
  ufw:
    rule: allow
    name: "Nginx Full"

- name: Firewall - Deny everything else
  ufw:
    state: enabled
    policy: deny
```

There is a lot to digest there. But the key is to become familiar with this format. All of those tasks look similar – some are performing some quite complex tasks, such as configuring a firewall. But Ansible's declarative format makes it clear what state the remote host should be in after this playbook has been run.

Taking a closer look at some of those modules:

```
- name: index.html also known as main.html
  file:
    state: link
    src: /var/www/html/index.html
    dest: /var/www/html/main.html
```

The file module can perform many actions on files and directories – adding, deleting, and setting ownership and permissions. In this case, it is being asked to ensure there is a link between the source and destination. This is a Linux concept where a link is essentially a shortcut to the original file; the correct name is symbolic link. When visiting the destination file main.html, you will actually be shown the content of the source file index.html.

```
- name: Update the website content
  lineinfile:
    path: /var/www/html/index.html
    line: "Just re-decorating a little!"
```

The lineinfile module can be used to declare that a line should or should not exist within a specific file. In this case, there is no state specified, so it takes the default value state: present. Most modules have sensible defaults for the most common actions. For example, we did not specify *where* in the file the line should be present, so by default lineinfile will insert it at the end of the file.

```
- name: Firewall - Allow SSH connections
  ufw:
    rule: allow
    name: OpenSSH
```

Finally, we use the ufw module. UFW (Uncomplicated Firewall) is a simple firewall provided by Ubuntu servers which is designed to be easy to maintain. This Ansible module makes it a breeze – these tasks add a couple of rules to the firewall to allow OpenSSH and nginx through the firewall and then start the firewall in a default mode of Deny everything else. This should result in the web server only allowing connections via SSH (as that is used by Ansible to manage the host) and web traffic in blocking everything else.

Let's run this playbook; the output should be familiar by now:

```
> ansible-playbook webservers.yml

PLAY [webservers] ****

TASK [Gathering Facts] ****
ok: [web-002.local]
ok: [web-001.local]

TASK [Ensure nginx is installed] ****
ok: [web-002.local]
ok: [web-001.local]

TASK [Push website content to the web root] ****
ok: [web-001.local]
ok: [web-002.local]

TASK [index.html also known as main.html] ****
changed: [web-002.local]
changed: [web-001.local]

TASK [Update the website content] ****
changed: [web-002.local]
changed: [web-001.local]

TASK [Firewall - Allow SSH connections] ****
changed: [web-001.local]
changed: [web-002.local]

TASK [Firewall - Allow website connections] ****
changed: [web-001.local]
changed: [web-002.local]

TASK [Firewall - Deny everything else] ****
changed: [web-001.local]
changed: [web-002.local]
```

To prove that worked as expected, visit the new main.html via your web browser – if you can reach it, then the firewall has allowed your connection through as expected:

```
http://web-001.local/main.html
```

If you are unable to reach the site via that URL, please try

```
http://192.168.98.111/main.html
```

Summary

This chapter introduced a variety of modules, why and how they work, and how you can leverage so much power from Ansible's simple declarative playbook format.

We deep dived into a single module, apt, to really understand how we can manipulate the arguments passed into a module to instruct it to take the exact actions we intended. We saw how module arguments are declarative, and we express the state that we want the module to put the server into rather than telling it how to get there. The module itself already contains the logic to figure out the if and how.

Once familiar with apt, we created a new playbook designed to upgrade all of the packages on our remote hosts and then reboot them – introducing a couple of new modules showing just how simple it is to reboot a server and wait for it to be online again before continuing. This can be extended to many use cases, using similar modules that can wait for specific network events or files to be created.

Finally, we extended the simple webservers.yml playbook to include a lot more tasks. Each of these tasks uses a module, and each module has one area of expertise which it carries out dutifully. We saw how simple it can be to manage something as complex as a firewall and how we can modify files on the server with a simple file or lineinfile task. There are hundreds of modules available, too many to memorize. When you need to do something with Ansible, go searching on their website – there is almost always a module to achieve what you want.

Optional Excercise: Exploring "apt latest" Idempotence

To explore the lack of idempotence when using state: latest in our apt modules, we will first build a slightly more advanced playbook. Each task will not be explored in detail, but the output will hopefully speak for itself.

Create a new playbook named `apt-latest.yml`:

```
---
- hosts: web-001.local
  become: true
  tasks:
    - name: Ensure nginx is installed
      apt:
        name: nginx
        state: present
        cache_valid_time: 60

    - name: Determine nginx start time
      systemd:
        name: nginx
        state: started
      check: true
      register: nginx

    - name: Print current nginx start time
      debug:
        msg:"{{nginx.status.ExecMainStartTimestamp}}"
```

```
- name: Add nginx PPA with more recent version
  apt_repository:
    repo: ppa:nginx/stable

- name: Ensure nginx is latest (cause upgrade)
  apt:
    name: nginx
    state: latest
    update_cache: yes

- name: Determine nginx start time
  systemd:
    name: nginx
    state: started
  check: true
  register: nginx

- name: Print current nginx start time
  debug:
    msg:"{{nginx.status.ExecMainStartTimestamp}}"
```

Run the preceding playbook and observe the output from the tasks named "Print current nginx start time." We expect nginx to be installed and running after the first few tasks, then add a new apt repository (a source for installing packages using apt) which contains a newer version of nginx than the one currently installed. The next task will ensure the *latest* version of nginx is installed, causing an upgrade, and finally we print the start time again.

The following output from this playbook shows that the start time of nginx does indeed change, proving that state: latest, as its name would suggest, results in a restart of the service:

```
> ansible-playbook apt-latest.yml

PLAY [web-001.local] ****

TASK [Gathering Facts] ****
ok: [web-001.local]

TASK [Ensure nginx is installed] ****
ok: [web-001.local]

TASK [Determine nginx start time] ****
ok: [web-001.local]

TASK [Print current nginx start time] ****
ok: [web-001.local] =>
  msg: Wed 2020-07-29 10:48:34 UTC

TASK [Add nginx PPA with more recent version] ****
changed: [web-001.local]

TASK [Ensure nginx is latest (cause upgrade)] ****
changed: [web-001.local]

TASK [Determine nginx start time] ****
ok: [web-001.local]

TASK [Print current nginx start time] ****
ok: [web-001.local] =>
  msg: Wed 2020-07-29 10:49:09 UTC

PLAY RECAP ****
web-001.local : ok=8 changed=2 unreachable=0 failed=0
```

CHAPTER 6

It's All Variable, That's a Fact!

We are building up a good foundation for what Ansible is all about and how it fits together. Back in Chapter 3 while talking about inventories, we touched on the concept of *variables* – defining a variable named http_port with a value of 8080 to the group of hosts referred to as webservers. Since then, that variable has not been used, as there has been no obvious use case – but as the complexity of the playbook increases, it will become apparent that variables are of major importance, especially when structuring the playbooks.

Why not simply hardcode this into the playbook or configuration file which is pushed to the server(s) using Ansible? That may well work for web servers which all run on port 8080 – but how about the load balancer, which should be on 80?

As admirable a goal of making all our systems reproducible is, there are of course always going to be these differences between them. We can limit those differences by ensuring consistent OS and package versions, but ultimately things like IP addresses, hostnames, configuration for load balancers, etc. will always need to be unique. Hardcoding such configuration information into our playbooks would quickly become complicated. For that, Ansible offers variables. In short, tasks define the

© Shaun R Smith and Peter Membrey 2022
S. R. Smith and P. Membrey, *Beginning Ansible Concepts and Application*,
https://doi.org/10.1007/978-1-4842-8173-4_6

state of the system (what is installed, where config files live, which services are running), while variables help deal with the *differences* between systems (configuration files, IP addresses, hostnames).

Years ago, I (Pete) had a rather unfortunate experience planning a family holiday. Given the Internet is a thing, and things are in general cheaper online, I decided to take care of my family's holiday bookings myself. I arranged everything – the taxi pickups, the flights, and of course the hotel – and I saved quite a bit of money. I was quite pleased with myself, a feeling that was rather short-lived. Due to an issue at work, I had to change my holiday plans, but no matter, it was easy enough to update everything online to be one week early – except I'd forgotten to update the taxi company who was going to take us to the airport. Needless to say, there was no taxi to pick us up, and by the time I'd sorted that out, we'd missed our flight. Fortunately, I was able to get another flight within a few hours, but as I was under just a teensy bit of stress (stress not being conducive to clear thought), it didn't occur to me to update the pickup service or the hotel. Thus, we landed with no pickup service, and by the time we eventually got to the hotel, they'd cancelled our booking. It goes without saying that was a very expensive and painful learning experience.

Last year, I had to do the same thing, but to avoid a cold sweat, I took advantage of my credit card's concierge service to book everything. Then, once again, I had to make a change, but when I called the concierge, they assured me that they would contact everyone involved and that everything was fine. The holiday went without a hitch, and because I wasn't trying to be clever, the whole journey was stress-free (mostly). There are a lot of benefits to having things in one place!

What does this have to do with variables?

Consider the preceding story but in terms of your production infrastructure. You need to change some attribute of the service; perhaps you're having to migrate to a new provider, and so your IP addresses all change, or perhaps you replace one service with another and need port changes. You go through the playbook and update it. Deploy. Your entire site goes down. What went wrong? We forgot to also update the firewall rules, the glue configuration for the services that talk to one another, etc.

This is where variables can save the day – your personal concierge. Set the value for one thing such as the IP address of the database in one place and use it throughout your playbooks.

Defining Variables and Precedence

Variables can be defined in many different locations within your Ansible playbooks, and it is important to understand the precedence (or priority) that each gets to avoid confusion. We will not cover all of them here, as that would be jumping ahead a lot. Instead, we will cover the most common practices for defining variables in a simple playbook: host vars, playbook vars, and group vars.

As the names suggest, each type of variable is assigned to a different attribute: the host itself, the playbook, or the group of hosts, as defined in our inventory. Moreover, host vars and group vars can be declared in line with the inventory, as we saw in Chapter 3, or externally in special directories. The more specific you become, the higher precedence a variable has, meaning it will overwrite a variable with the same name from a lower precedence location, similar to how the later declaration in an inventory file will override an earlier one. This is best understood with an example.

Open the inventory file `inventory/webservers` for review:

```
---
webservers:
  hosts:
    web-001.local:
    web-002:
        ansible_host: 192.168.98.112
  vars:
    http_port: 8080
```

In this example, http_port is defined inside the *inventory file*, under the *group* webservers, making this a *group variable*.

As a reminder from Chapter 3, explore this variable:

```
> ansible -m debug -a "var=http_port" all

web-002 | SUCCESS => {
    "http_port": 8080
}
lb-001.local | SUCCESS => {
    "http_port": "VARIABLE IS NOT DEFINED!"
}
web-001.local | SUCCESS => {
    "http_port": 8080
}
```

The variable is applied to the two hosts that belong to the webservers group and is not defined for the host belonging to the load_balancers group, as expected.

What would happen then if we were to define that same variable, but with a different value somewhere else? Let's go ahead and create a group_vars directory – this can live alongside your inventory (recommended) or your playbook:

```
> mkdir inventory/group_vars/
```

Now create a new file named all inside the inventory/group_vars/ directory with the following content:

```
> vi inventory/group_vars/all

---

http_port: 80
```

The first line, three dashes (---), is a YAML directive to declare the start of a YAML document. We do not need to worry about why that is there for our use of YAML – but it's worth knowing that it is deliberate.

This sets the same variable http_port to a different value than previously to show precedence, meaning which one wins. To find out:

```
> ansible -m debug -a "var=http_port" all

lb-001.local | SUCCESS => {
    "http_port": 80
}
web-002 | SUCCESS => {
    "http_port": 80
}
web-001.local | SUCCESS => {
    "http_port": 80
}
```

Well, that is different. It would seem the http_port in group_vars/ all takes precedence over the group vars defined in the inventory file, but something else changed too. The load balancer host now also has a value for http_port.

That is because the file we created in the group_vars directory had the filename all. Remember, all is an implicit group within Ansible that will always contain *all* the hosts in the inventory. This is a great way of defining a default variable value that will apply to all hosts unless a value with higher precedence is provided.

In this example, the webservers should have a different `http_port` than the load balancer – so create a new file under the `inventory/group_vars` directory named `webservers` (the name should match the target group):

```
---
http_port: 8080
```

Running the same command again should show that the **more specific** group variables take *precedence* over the more general `all` group variables:

```
> ansible -m debug -a "var=http_port" all

lb-001.local | SUCCESS => {
    "http_port": 80
}
web-002 | SUCCESS => {
    "http_port": 8080
}
web-001.local | SUCCESS => {
    "http_port": 8080
}
```

Perfect. The more specifically targeted the group becomes, the higher the precedence. As you might imagine, we can be more specific still than the group. A host variable will always be more specific than a group variable – so modifying the port for a single host would win over all of this. Jumping back to `inventory/webservers`, modify the host variable for web-002 and set the `http_port` to 1234:

```
---
webservers:
  hosts:
    web-001.local:
    web-002:
```

```
        ansible_host: 192.168.98.112
        http_port: 1234
    vars:
        http_port: 8080
```

Then run the same command again:

```
> ansible -m debug -a "var=http_port" all
web-002 | SUCCESS => {
    "http_port": 1234
}
web-001.local | SUCCESS => {
    "http_port": 8080
}
lb-001.local | SUCCESS => {
    "http_port": 80
}
```

That in a nutshell is variable precedence. The more specifically defined the variable is (meaning the closer it is to being linked to a single entity), the higher its precedence. In simple terms, task vars are more specific than playbook, which is more specific than host, which is more specific than group, which is more specific than implicit group, and so on. This may seem very confusing at first – but as you play with variables more, you will quickly get the hang of it. For more information, you can always consult "Variable Precedence Hierarchy."

Changing the HTTP Port

To bring us back on track, simplify inventory/webservers by removing the original http_port which is no longer relevant and bringing web-002 in line with web-001:

```
---
webservers:
  hosts:
    web-001.local:
    web-002.local:
```

To verify everything is as it should be, compare your output:

```
> ansible -m debug -a "var=http_port" all

lb-001.local | SUCCESS => {
    "http_port": 80
}
web-002.local | SUCCESS => {
    "http_port": 8080
}
web-001.local | SUCCESS => {
    "http_port": 8080
}
```

Testing Your Change

Changing the HTTP port of your running web server could be considered a risky change. There are many things that might go wrong. Perhaps, the configuration is bad, or perhaps the web service does not come back up on the expected port. Therefore, let's add a simple test to the playbook **before** changing the port. While we are there, we will remove some tasks that were designed to get familiar with various modules.

Edit the webservers.yml playbook to make it resemble:

```
---
- hosts: webservers
  become: true
```

```
tasks:
  - name: Ensure nginx is installed
    apt:
      name: nginx
      state: present

  - name: Push website content to the web root
    copy:
      src: index.html
      dest: /var/www/html/
      mode: u=rw,g=r,o=r

  - name: Firewall - Allow SSH connections
    ufw:
      rule: allow
      name: OpenSSH

  - name: Firewall - Allow website connections
    ufw:
      rule: allow
      name: "Nginx Full"

  - name: Firewall - Deny everything else
    ufw:
      state: enabled
      policy: deny

  - name: Validate that the http_port is working
    wait_for:
      port: "{{ http_port }}"
      timeout: 5
```

This should not work right now, since it is using the http_port variable as defined using {{ http_port }} and we haven't updated our running nginx yet. That is important – we define a failing test case, then do the work to make the test case pass.

Those curly braces {{ }} are important; they tell Ansible that we are expecting a variable with this name to exist and to replace it with the value of the variable. Run this playbook to see what happens:

```
> ansible-playbook webservers.yml

PLAY [webservers] ****

TASK [Gathering Facts] ****
ok: [web-001.local]
ok: [web-002.local]

TASK [Ensure nginx is installed] ****
ok: [web-001.local]
ok: [web-002.local]

TASK [Push website content to the web root] ****
changed: [web-001.local]
changed: [web-002.local]

TASK [Firewall - Allow SSH connections] ****
ok: [web-001.local]
ok: [web-002.local]

TASK [Firewall - Allow website connections] ****
ok: [web-002.local]
ok: [web-001.local]

TASK [Firewall - Deny everything else] ****
ok: [web-002.local]
ok: [web-001.local]
```

TASK [Validate that the http_port is working] ****
```
fatal: [web-001.local]: FAILED! => changed=false
  elapsed: 5
  msg: Timeout when waiting for 127.0.0.1:8080
fatal: [web-002.local]: FAILED! => changed=false
  elapsed: 5
  msg: Timeout when waiting for 127.0.0.1:8080
```

Great. As expected, our test fails; as the webserver port has not yet been changed, the wait_for module is unable to connect to it on the http_port of 8080.

Let's modify the nginx port to use the http_port variable. For this, we will make use of the replace module – this searches for a regular expression within the file and replaces it with a new value. There are better ways of achieving this, which we will cover in a later chapter.

Insert the following tasks *between* those shown:

```
---
- hosts: webservers
  become: true
  tasks:
    - name: Ensure nginx is installed
      apt:
        name: nginx
        state: present

    - name: Change the nginx port
      replace:
        path: /etc/nginx/sites-enabled/default
        regexp: "listen [0-9]+"
        replace: "listen {{ http_port }}"
```

```
  - name: Reload nginx for new config
    service:
      name: nginx
      state: reloaded

  - name: Push website content to the web root
    copy:
      src: index.html
      dest: /var/www/html/
      mode: u=rw,g=r,o=r
```

`<truncated>`

These two tasks instruct ansible to replace the content in a configuration file with one containing the value of the http_port variable and then to reload the nginx service to pick up the configuration change. Clearly, this isn't idempotent – since every time we run the playbook, nginx will be restarted. We will fix that in a later chapter.

For now, let's run this playbook and see the port change:

```
> ansible-playbook webservers.yml

PLAY [webservers] ****

TASK [Gathering Facts] ****
ok: [web-002.local]
ok: [web-001.local]

TASK [Ensure nginx is installed] ****
ok: [web-001.local]
ok: [web-002.local]

TASK [Change the nginx port] ****
changed: [web-001.local]
changed: [web-002.local]
```

```
TASK [Reload nginx for new config] ****
changed: [web-002.local]
changed: [web-001.local]

TASK [Push website content to the web root] ****
changed: [web-001.local]
changed: [web-002.local]

TASK [Firewall - Allow SSH connections] ****
ok: [web-001.local]
ok: [web-002.local]

TASK [Firewall - Allow website connections] ****
ok: [web-001.local]
ok: [web-002.local]

TASK [Firewall - Deny everything else] ****
ok: [web-002.local]
ok: [web-001.local]
```

TASK [Validate that the http_port is working] ****
```
ok: [web-002.local]
ok: [web-001.local]
```

Great! This time after changing the port and reloading nginx, the test that we added earlier shows ok. That means everything is working just fine, right? Browse using the **new port** to find out:

```
http://web-001.local:8080/
```

or

```
http://192.168.98.111:8080/
```

Uh-oh. Seems something went wrong. The website does not load, just showing a timeout page:

The Firewall

What went wrong? We had a test in place to verify that nginx was working on the new port – it said everything was ok. Well, it is important to understand that every *task* in Ansible is run on the remote host and not from the view of the controller. wait_for in this case is actually running a module *on the web server itself* waiting for port 8080 to become available. Because the test is local to the web server, it does not pass through the firewall. Furthermore, because we hadn't used a variable from the start, when changing the http_port we forgot to also update the firewall rule – meaning the firewall is still blocking connections from the outside to port 8080.

This may feel contrived, but variations of it happen a lot. Especially as playbooks grow, becoming more complex, with many independent but interacting moving parts, the scope for such errors is huge. Even when we considered the failure case, we still got caught out by a bad test.

That is why we use variables for configuration and keep variability far away from the playbook's declaration of state.

Let's fix the test; modify the task to have the following lines:

```
- name: Validate that the http_port is working
  wait_for:
    host: "{{ ansible_host }}"
    port: "{{ http_port }}"
    timeout: 5
  connection: local
```

The first additional line tells wait_for to connect to a specific host to perform the check. Here, we have used a variable named ansible_host – that is a magic variable that always exists and has the value of the hostname or IP address that Ansible is using to communicate with the remote host. There are lots of magic variables available, some of which we will cover shortly.

The second additional line, connection: local, tells ansible that we want to run this particular task on the localhost – the machine running the ansible playbook – rather than on the remote host which would be the norm. Now wait_for will be going through the remote host's firewall to perform the check – let us rerun the playbook to see what happens:

```
<truncate>

TASK [Validate that the http_port is working] ****
fatal: [web-001.local]: FAILED! => changed=false
  elapsed: 6
  msg: Timeout when waiting for web-001.local:8080
fatal: [web-002.local]: FAILED! => changed=false
  elapsed: 6
  msg: Timeout when waiting for web-002.local:8080
```

Great. Now our test appears to be working and has picked up that we are unable to talk to web-001.local and web-002.local using port 8080 as expected. Time to fix the firewall rules using the http_port variable. Modify the task named Firewall - Allow website connections to use http_port rather than the provided Nginx Full rule:

```
- name: Firewall - Allow website connections
  ufw:
    rule: allow
    port: "{{ http_port }}"
```

Rerun the same playbook again; this time, the firewall should get updated using the new port, and the wait_for test should pass:

```
> ansible-playbook webservers.yml

PLAY [webservers] ****

TASK [Gathering Facts] ****
ok: [web-002.local]
ok: [web-001.local]

TASK [Ensure nginx is installed] ****
ok: [web-001.local]
ok: [web-002.local]

TASK [Change the nginx port] ****
ok: [web-002.local]
ok: [web-001.local]

TASK [Reload nginx for new config] ****
changed: [web-001.local]
changed: [web-002.local]

TASK [Push website content to the web root] ****
ok: [web-002.local]
ok: [web-001.local]
```

```
TASK [Firewall - Allow SSH connections] ****
ok: [web-002.local]
ok: [web-001.local]

TASK [Firewall - Allow website connections] ****
changed: [web-002.local]
changed: [web-001.local]

TASK [Firewall - Deny everything else] ****
ok: [web-002.local]
ok: [web-001.local]

TASK [Validate that the http_port is working] ****
ok: [web-001.local]
ok: [web-002.local]
```

That looks great. The firewall task made changes, since we modified it to use http_port, and the wait_for test passed. Now for the final validation, can it be reached via the web browser?

```
http://web-001.local:8080/
```

or

```
http://192.168.98.111:8080/
```

Variable Naming

You can be as descriptive as you like with your variable names; as in the preceding case, we used http_port. This name clearly defines what the purpose of the variable is – you should include as much context as needed in your variable names.

There are but two rules to follow:

1. Variables can include only letters, numbers, and underscores.

2. Variables **must** start with a letter, NOT a number or underscore.

If you follow those rules, Ansible will be happy with your variables. It is also important to understand that variables can contain various types of data. So far, we have only touched on a key-value pair variable – but Ansible also supports lists and dictionaries.

A list is a variable containing multiple values, which can be iterated over (more on that later!). For example, we may have a list of ports to enable through the firewall:

```
web_ports:
  - 80
  - 8080
  - 443
```

A dictionary on the other hand consists of nested variables and can contain any type beneath. These are already present in the form of the YAML inventory – that is a dictionary:

```
webservers:
  hosts:
    web-001.local:
    web-002.local:
    http_port: 1234
```

You can refer to specific values within a dictionary structure using the same format used in Python and other programming languages. For example, if we wanted to know the http_port for web-002.local, we could use

```
webservers['hosts']['web-002.local']['http_port']
```

This can be confusing, but it will become more intuitive as you see and use it more in the coming chapters.

Magic Variables

There are a number of variables that are defined as magic in Ansible. This essentially means that the variables will always exist, and they will magically have a value to reflect the internal state of Ansible. These variables cannot be set directly – if you attempt to assign a value to one of these magic variables, Ansible will override it. As a result, *most* begin with the prefix `ansible_`, but not all.

We can use these magic variables in our playbooks, just as we would any other variable – meaning from within our playbook we can understand Ansible's internal state. Consider that we got a new server from a data center, with a default hostname of `Ubuntu`. We would want to set the hostname of the remote host to match that in the Ansible inventory file, rather than manually logging into the host to change the hostname. Using a magic variable `inventory_hostname`, this is easy to achieve across *all* our hosts:

```
- name: Set the remote hostname
  hostname:
    name: "{{ inventory_hostname }}"
```

The utility of more magic variables will become clear as we progress through the following chapters. We might, for example, control whether or not a task is executed based on the host's membership to a particular group (such as staging or production). We may need to find some information about another host in the inventory, such as the IP address of the web servers to configure the load balancer.

All of this is made possible by using magic variables.

It's a Fact!

In addition to variables and magic variables, Ansible provides another type of variable that you may have heard of already – facts. While we have not made use of *facts* yet, you may recall that the first task of every playbook includes an implicit (meaning not something we added) task called *Gathering Facts*. As the name implies, this is Ansible gathering facts about the remote host.

Facts are things that are known to be true about the current host that Ansible is operating against. They are automatically gathered during the *Gathering Facts* task by a module named setup and include information that Ansible has learned about the host itself – things Ansible could not have known before it had connected to the host. This includes information such as the type and version of the operating system, the amount of RAM, network and disk configuration, and many other facts about the host.

To understand what these facts look like, let's run the setup module directly using an ad hoc command:

```
> ansible -m setup web-001.local

web-001.local | SUCCESS => {
    "ansible_facts": {
        "ansible_all_ipv4_addresses": [
            "10.0.2.15",
            "192.168.98.111"
        ],
        "ansible_all_ipv6_addresses": [
            "fe80::d0:42ff:fe45:d944",
            "fe80::a00:27ff:feaf:cb04"
        ],
        "ansible_apparmor": {
            "status": "enabled"
        },
```

```
    "ansible_architecture": "x86_64",
    "ansible_bios_date": "12/01/2006",
    "ansible_bios_version": "VirtualBox",
    "ansible_cmdline": {
        "BOOT_IMAGE": "/boot/vmlinuz-4.15.0-101-generic",
        "console": "ttyS0",
        "ro": true,
        "root": "LABEL=cloudimg-rootfs"
    }
}
```

The output from this command is long and will scroll off the screen quickly; feel free to scroll up to investigate, or pipe the output to the less command if you are comfortable doing so: ansible -m setup web-001.local | less

Let's take a snapshot and examine what we are looking at:

```
web-001.local | SUCCESS => {
    "ansible_facts": {
        "ansible_all_ipv4_addresses": [
            "10.0.2.15",
            "192.168.98.111"
        ],
        "ansible_distribution": "Ubuntu",
        "ansible_distribution_major_version": "18",
        "ansible_distribution_release": "bionic",
        "ansible_distribution_version": "18.04",
    }
}
```

Here, you can start to understand more about the remote host that Ansible is talking to – you could include this information into your configuration files or even conditionally run tasks based on the operating system type and version.

Note how the facts are returned from the `setup` module in the form of a large dictionary with the top-level key (bold) being called `ansible_facts`. This is a special key that tells Ansible to incorporate all the values into its known *facts* for this host. The setup module is not doing anything magical – it is simply gathering a lot of information on the remote host and then returning it to Ansible via the special variable `ansible_facts`. In fact, by returning the `ansible_facts` dictionary, **any** module can return additional facts that will be incorporated into the known facts for the host. For example, take a closer look at the output from the hostname change we ran in Chapter 5:

```
web-001 | SUCCESS => {
    "ansible_facts": {
        "ansible_domain": "",
        "ansible_fqdn": "web-001",
        "ansible_hostname": "web-001",
        "ansible_nodename": "web-001"
    },
    "changed": false,
    "name": "web-001 "
}
```

The hostname module is returning its own `ansible_facts`, which will be incorporated into the current facts about the remote host. In this case, the `hostname` module has just changed the hostname, meaning the original `ansible_facts` relating to the hostname will be inaccurate, unless the `hostname` module updates them. That is exactly what it does.

Using Facts

Using a fact is as simple as using a variable, and facts are globally scoped, meaning they are available anywhere within your playbooks. Imagine we run multiple servers with different operating systems (we wouldn't generally choose to, but legacy systems do exist). You may need a different set of Ansible tasks for different operating systems – especially with package names and different firewall technologies.

To achieve that, you might use the fact named `ansible_distribution`, which tells you the Linux distribution that is running – such as Ubuntu, Debian, and Red Hat. In this example, we set the hostname of the server to use the distribution name:

```
- name: Set the remote hostname
  hostname:
    name: "{{ ansible_distribution }}-001"
```

To understand all the built-in facts available to you, simply use the preceding command `ansible -m setup web-001` to list them, replacing `web-001` with the relevant hostname.

Disabling Fact Gathering

Sometimes, you may not want facts to be automatically gathered for a host. Fact gathering can take time, many seconds for some remote hosts, when operating against thousands of hosts that can really add up to long delays. If your playbook does not rely on any of the facts gathered by the `setup` module, then you can *disable* it from being run automatically. A great example would be where you just want to change a configuration file and conditionally reload a service – no facts needed.

One place we might want this would be the upgrade.yml playbook – which simply does not rely on these facts at all:

```
---
- hosts: web-001.local
  become: true
  gather_facts: no
  tasks:
    - name: Upgrade all packages
      apt:
        upgrade: dist
        update_cache: yes

    - name: Reboot the host
      reboot:
```

If we were to run this playbook again now, we would notice that the implicit "Gathering Facts" task that we have become so familiar with at the start of the play is no longer there. That is one less SSH connection, and one less execution on the remote host.

The whole playbook completes faster as a result, especially if those remote hosts are globally distributed across slow links.

Register Your Success

There will inevitably be some interaction between various tasks in your playbooks. Imagine you are headed to the shops to buy some groceries, but you have no cash in your purse. The local grocery store hasn't yet heard of mobile payments such as Apple Pay, so first you need to stop by the ATM to withdraw some cash, so that you can pay for your groceries.

You turn up at the ATM, push in your card, enter your PIN, and

"Error: The service is unavailable at this time"

You did not get the cash. You do not get groceries. There is a **dependency** here: without the cash, there is simply no point in going to the grocery store. Yet that is exactly what our upgrade.yml playbook is doing. It is visiting the grocery store without knowing if it got the cash or not. It is rebooting the remote host every time it is run, regardless of whether packages were upgraded or a reboot is even required.

To fix that, we can share information between tasks, just as we understand the link between getting cash and buying groceries. We can **register** the result from one task, meaning to put the result into a variable; and we can then refer to that variable in another independent task to create a link between them. In this case, we would register the result of the apt upgrade task and refer to that variable in the reboot task.

The debug module can be used to inspect the value of the registered variable, helping us understand better how it might be used. The reboot task should be deleted for the time being, else you will spend a lot of time waiting for the host to reboot.

Let's make those changes now:

```
---
- hosts: web-001.local
  become: true
  gather_facts: no
  tasks:
    - name: Upgrade all packages
      apt:
        upgrade: dist
        update_cache: yes
      register: upgrade_result

    - name: Inspect upgrade_result
      debug:
        var: upgrade_result
```

Caution   Be careful with indentation. The register keyword is in line with name: and apt: (the module name) as it is a function of the task itself, not of the module.

Run this playbook and inspect the output:

```
> ansible-playbook upgrade.yml

PLAY [web-001.local] ****

TASK [Upgrade all packages] ****
ok: [web-001.local]

TASK [Inspect upgrade_result] ****
ok: [web-001.local] =>
  upgrade_result:
    changed: false
    failed: false
    msg: |-
      Reading package lists...
      Building dependency tree...
      Reading state information...
      Calculating upgrade...
      0 upgraded, 0 newly installed, 0 to remove and 0 not
      upgraded.
    stderr: ''
    stderr_lines: []
    stdout: |-
      Reading package lists...
      Building dependency tree...
      Reading state information...
      Calculating upgrade...
```

```
    0 upgraded, 0 newly installed, 0 to remove and 0 not
    upgraded.
  stdout_lines:
  - Reading package lists...
  - Building dependency tree...
  - Reading state information...
  - Calculating upgrade...
  - 0 upgraded, 0 newly installed, 0 to remove and 0 not
    upgraded.
```

The upgrade_result variable now contains a familiar looking set of variables: changed, failed, stderr, stdout, and so on. The registered variable contains all the key-value pairs that you see from the module itself when running Ansible in *verbose* mode.

Knowing that we now have access not only to the entire output of the module but to those critical ansible result variables, changed and failed, we can now fix the dependency between *upgrading* and *rebooting*. We should only reboot when upgrades have happened or when the apt module reports that the task changed the remote host:

```
---
- hosts: web-001.local
  become: true
  gather_facts: no
  tasks:
    - name: Upgrade all packages
      apt:
        upgrade: dist
        update_cache: yes
      register: upgrade_result
```

```
- name: Reboot the host
  reboot:
  when: upgrade_result.changed
```

when: is a special keyword for a task which makes the task conditional, meaning it will only run when the when: statement is true. We will cover this in more detail in a future chapter.

The result is that when we run this playbook, the reboot task will only be run **if** the upgrade task made changes:

```
> ansible-playbook upgrade.yml

PLAY [web-001.local] ****

TASK [Upgrade all packages] ****
ok: [web-001.local]

TASK [Reboot the host] ****
skipping: [web-001.local]
```

We can see that when the upgrade task returns ok, meaning nothing needed to be updated, the reboot task is *skipped*. If you did have updates applied, wait for the playbook to finish (meaning reboot has completed) and run it again immediately. This time, there should be no updates applied, and your output should be similar.

Summary

That was a lot to take in. We have walked through defining our own variables and where to define them. Variable precedence is especially important in the Ansible ecosystem, and understanding which variables override others can be a huge asset allowing you to set sensible defaults at the global level, which can be overridden by specific hosts or playbooks further down the line.

Once the http_port was correctly dialed in and variable precedence was working as expected, the webservers.yml playbook was updated to make use of the http_port for nginx configuration. There was a test case in place to verify that this happened as expected, only it didn't work quite as expected. It was shown that all tasks are executed on the remote host, and testing a web server's reachability from the host itself doesn't always capture the full picture. In this case, nginx was working perfectly fine on the new port, but the firewall was still configured to only allow connections on the now-unused port.

Using the http_port variable allows you to configure the port in one central location and set up the playbooks to configure all of the necessary components in the path to make sure that port change does not impact your overall system. Imagine in future you have a load balancer pointed at those web servers; changing the web port requires not only nginx and firewall changes but also changes to the load balancer's configuration. Managing such changes using variables can reduce the risk of bugs.

Then we talked about some important bookkeeping topics such as how to name your variables. Ansible has few, clear, requirements for variable naming – and if you stick to them, then your variables will work as expected. There are also several *magic variables* in ansible – things that Ansible understands about its internal state, but that are not learned from the remote hosts (those would be *facts*), such as the hostnames that are used in the inventory to tell Ansible how to connect to the host or the username used to connect to the host.

We then moved on to one of the most useful set of variables, *facts*! You will come to love facts throughout your journey, especially if you get into the management of network or disk configuration. We saw how you can use facts in your own playbooks and that facts are dynamic – every module that runs on the host has the ability to return additional facts to Ansible. When you are comfortable playing with modules, there are several fact gathering modules available, such as ec2_metadata_facts for gathering metadata from AWS EC2 instances and importing the information into Ansible facts.

Sometimes, it is useful to disable the automate fact gathering task at the start of each playbook run, especially when your playbook does not rely on any facts at all. This is often the case for short maintenance type playbooks, such as upgrade.yml, and can improve the runtime of playbooks, especially when run against 1000s of hosts.

Finally, we saw how to communicate status between tasks using the register: keyword. This allows us to read the status of one task during execution of another, so that we don't go to the grocery store without getting any cash.

Finally, remember they are all just variables!

Variable Precedence Hierarchy

Variable precedence, in ascending order of precedence. The higher number in the list denotes high precedence, meaning the items toward the bottom will always override the same named variables from those lower-numbered items:

1. Command-line values (e.g., "-u user")

2. Role defaults

3. Inventory file or script group vars

4. Inventory group_vars/all

5. Playbook group_vars/all

6. Inventory group_vars/*

7. Playbook group_vars/*

8. Inventory file or script host vars

9. Inventory host_vars/*

10. Playbook host_vars/*

11. Host facts/cached set_facts

12. Play vars

13. Play vars_prompt

14. Play vars_files

15. Role vars (defined in role/vars/main.yml)

16. Block vars (only for tasks in block)

17. Task vars (only for the task)

18. include_vars

19. set_facts/registered vars

20. Role (and include_role) params

21. Include params

22. Extra vars (always win precedence)

Source: https://docs.ansible.com/ansible/latest/user_guide/
playbooks_variables.html

CHAPTER 7

Becoming an Ansible Jinja

We have hinted a lot at configuration files and the ability to use centralized variables across multiple configuration files. We have pushed some custom static website content to our web servers and viewed it through a web browser.

But what ties all these things together? *How* do we use a variable inside our web content or add the http_port into our nginx configuration file to ensure the web server is really on port 8080?

Enter Jinja2.

Jinja2 is a powerful templating language which allows you to effectively separate configuration (website files, configuration files) from process (where those files should be placed, what services should be installed and running). It enables us to group important content together in one place.

Take, for example, the previous example where we pushed some static website content to the host and then used the lineinfile module to modify it in place. That is not very declarative, as we essentially created a procedural program to push the initial content and then modify it with another Ansible task. They must run in a specific order and define explicit actions, not a final desired state. It is extremely difficult to look at such a playbook and understand what the end state of our host might look like.

© Shaun R Smith and Peter Membrey 2022
S. R. Smith and P. Membrey, *Beginning Ansible Concepts and Application*,
https://doi.org/10.1007/978-1-4842-8173-4_7

Jinja2 and the Ansible `template` module allow you to separate the website content from tasks by creating what is called a template file. The format of these template files is Jinja2.

In the beginning, your template file will mostly be your content: plaintext configuration files, HTML files, etc. But over time you will start to replace static parts of the configuration with dynamic data such as variables, conditional logic (if statements), and even looping over multiple data points to generate configuration elements – bringing more flexibility and power. Being in a single template file, it is very easy to see what the end result will look like and very intuitive to modify a file that is structured exactly as the end result would be.

In fact, in the production environments we operate today, our entire firewall configuration for thousands of dynamic services is defined via a single Jinja2 template – making it very easy for new developers to jump in and understand how the firewall is structured.

Variables and Jinja2

The previous chapter introduced variables and how to use them in your playbooks. We came across this strange format for variables, using curly braces surrounding the variable name: `{{ http_port }}`.

It was not obvious at the time, but this is Jinja2 in action. Ansible uses Jinja2 in many places, especially when dealing with variables, as it provides a huge set of features for empowering the humble variable. In this case, the "`{{ }}`" is an instruction to Jinja2 to interpret whatever appears inside as an *expression* that will be printed in place of everything, including the curly braces. You can think of this as Jinja2's `print` statement. It can be as simple as printing a variable, but we can also include math or logic inside the expression. We can get a lot more creative by knowing that this variable substitution is being carried out by a powerful templating engine with lots of great functionality. It is not a simple variable substitution.

Filters

One of the most common features used from Jinja2 in Ansible is filters. Filters allow you to *find* data inside large lists or dictionaries (such as those in ansible_facts) and *transform* the values from variables at the time you use them. There are a lot of filters available, over 50 at the time of writing, all of which perform a single action on a variable: be it replacing some content; converting the value to upper- or lowercase; rounding a number; finding the min, max, or sum from a list of numbers; sorting a list of elements alphabetically; or sanitizing strings to make them safe for certain operations such as URL parsing.

Multiple filters can be applied to a single variable in series. This is achieved through what we call piping – passing the *output* from one operation as the *input* to the next. This is just like piping in Linux; in fact, Jinja2 uses the same pipe character (|) to achieve it.

Let's look at an example of filters in action. Using the magic variable that we looked at earlier, {{ inventory_hostname }}, we can ensure that this is always uppercase.

Create a new playbook named hostname.yml:

```
---
- hosts: webservers
  become: true
  gather_facts: no
  tasks:
    - name: Raw value for inventory_hostname
      debug:
        msg: "{{ inventory_hostname }}"

    - name: Uppercase inventory_hostname
      debug:
        msg: "{{ inventory_hostname | upper }}"
```

```
- name: Raw value for inventory_hostname
  debug:
    msg: "{{ inventory_hostname }}"
```

There are three tasks defined, all using the debug module to print a message. That message includes a variable using the Jinja2 variable format introduced previously, except the second task uses a *pipe* to pass the output of the inventory_hostname variable as input to a function called upper.

Run this playbook and observe the output of the three tasks:

```
> ansible-playbook hostname.yml

PLAY [webservers] ****

TASK [Raw value for inventory_hostname] ****
ok: [web-001.local] =>
  msg: web-001.local
ok: [web-002.local] =>
  msg: web-002.local

TASK [Uppercase inventory_hostname] ****
ok: [web-001.local] =>
  msg: WEB-001.LOCAL
ok: [web-002.local] =>
  msg: WEB-002.LOCAL

TASK [Raw value for inventory_hostname] ****
ok: [web-001.local] =>
  msg: web-001.local
ok: [web-002.local] =>
  msg: web-002.local
```

The msg: output from the debug module for the Uppercase inventory_
hostname task has been converted to all UPPERCASE characters – this was
achieved by the upper filter that was applied to the variable in the playbook.

An important thing to note is the result of the final task, where we print
the raw value of inventory_hostname for the second time. The value is
still in lowercase, as defined in the inventory. The filter that was applied to
inventory_hostname in the second task was applied **only** to that instance
of the variable. The variable's value is transformed before being output, but
the actual variable remains unchanged.

We can pipe as many filters as we need onto the variable; each would
be applied in turn. A rather pointless example of this would be to convert
the hostname to uppercase and then back to lowercase. Modify the filter in
the hostname.yml playbook to match this:

```
- name: Uppercase inventory_hostname
  debug:
    msg: "{{ inventory_hostname | upper | lower }}"
```

And rerun the playbook:

```
> ansible-playbook hostname.yml

TASK [Uppercase inventory_hostname] ****
ok: [web-001.local] =>
  msg: web-001.local
ok: [web-002.local] =>
  msg: web-002.local
```

It is a pointless change, but it makes filter piping clear. First, the variable
value was passed as input to the upper function, which converts the string
to uppercase as we previously saw; the output from the upper function was
then passed as input to the lower function, which converts the string to
lowercase again. There are no more filters applied after this, so the output is
the result after the final filter – in this case, a lowercase hostname.

The default( ) Filter

Often when using variables, it can be desirable to provide a default value at the time of use. This ensures that even if the variable is later not defined for whatever reason, the playbook will not become broken. A great example where this would be useful is our http_port. Right now, we are relying on the group_vars/all file to set the default, but that means our playbook itself is not easily reusable. If we gave that playbook to somebody else, they would also need to add the http_port as a variable somewhere in their Ansible project; otherwise, the playbook would fail to execute due to an undefined variable.

Setting a default value for http_port is useful, but we won't be able to see the results without removing all our hard work with variables earlier, so instead let us add a new feature: the nginx status page. The status page can live at any URL of your choosing, but we should default to something sensible.

Open up the webservers.yml playbook once again, and let's add a new task to add status page configuration **before** the task to Reload nginx for new config:

```
---
- hosts: webservers
  become: true
  tasks:
    - name: Ensure nginx is installed
      apt:
        name: nginx
        state: present

    - name: Change the nginx port
      replace:
        path: /etc/nginx/sites-enabled/default
        regexp: "listen [0-9]+"
```

```
    replace: "listen {{http_port | default(80)}}"

- name: Ensure nginx status is enabled
  blockinfile:
    path: /etc/nginx/sites-enabled/default
    insertafter: "^server {"
    block: |
      location /{{ status_url }} {
        stub_status on;
      }

- name: Reload nginx for new config
  service:
    name: nginx
    state: reloaded

<truncated>
```

Note   The character following block: in the new task is a pipe (|).
This tells YAML that what follows is a multiline value. The multiline
value ends when the indentation ends, as with everything in YAML.

We are using another new module named blockinfile, like
lineinfile, only this module allows you to provide a whole block of text to
insert. We have also introduced a new variable {{ status_url }}, but so
far we have not actually defined this anywhere.

Let's run the playbook and see what happens:

```
> ansible-playbook webservers.yml

PLAY [webservers] ****

TASK [Gathering Facts] ****
```

```
ok: [web-002.local]
ok: [web-001.local]

TASK [Ensure nginx is installed] ****
ok: [web-002.local]
ok: [web-001.local]

TASK [Change the nginx port] ****
ok: [web-002.local]
ok: [web-001.local]

TASK [Ensure nginx status is enabled] ****
fatal: [web-001.local]: FAILED! =>
  msg: |-
    The task includes an option with an undefined variable. The
    error was: 'status_url' is undefined

    The error appears to be in 'webservers.yml': line 16,
    column 7, but may be elsewhere in the file depending on the
    exact syntax problem.

    The offending line appears to be:

      - name: Ensure nginx status is enabled
        ^ here

    <truncated>
```

We got an error; the new task failed. The error message that Ansible printed shows that the variable status_url which we tried to use is *undefined,* meaning no value has been set for this variable. In practice, one would hope the playbook could work with sensible defaults.

Open webservers.yml again, and modify that variable to add a default value that makes sense, in this case 'status':

```
- name: Ensure nginx status is enabled
  blockinfile:
    path: /etc/nginx/sites-enabled/default
    insertafter: "^server {"
    block: |
      location /{{status_url | default('status')}} {
        stub_status on;
      }
```

Now run the same playbook again, with a default filter applied to the undefined variable:

```
> ansible-playbook webservers.yml

PLAY [webservers] ****

TASK [Gathering Facts] ****
ok: [web-002.local]
ok: [web-001.local]

TASK [Ensure nginx is installed] ****
ok: [web-002.local]
ok: [web-001.local]

TASK [Change the nginx port] ****
ok: [web-002.local]
ok: [web-001.local]

TASK [Ensure nginx status is enabled] ****
changed: [web-002.local]
changed: [web-001.local]
```

```
TASK [Reload nginx for new config] ****
changed: [web-002.local]
changed: [web-001.local]

TASK [Push website content to the web root] ****
ok: [web-002.local]
ok: [web-001.local]

TASK [Firewall - Allow SSH connections] ****
ok: [web-002.local]
ok: [web-001.local]

TASK [Firewall - Allow website connections] ****
ok: [web-001.local]
ok: [web-002.local]

TASK [Firewall - Deny everything else] ****
ok: [web-002.local]
ok: [web-001.local]

TASK [Validate that the http_port is working] ****
ok: [web-002.local]
ok: [web-001.local]
```

Everything seems to have worked as expected. Our default filter recovered from the error seen in the previous run. Let's ensure that the nginx status page is indeed available at the default URL /status:

```
http://web-001.local:8080/status/
```

or

```
http://192.168.98.111:8080/status/
```

Templating

So Jinja2 has filters, and they are very powerful – we can manipulate strings, lists, and dictionaries in many ways, set default values, and even combine multiple filters together in series. But that is just the starting point for Jinja2. Where it really shines is as a *templating* language, and that is not lost on Ansible.

Templating allows you to keep your content and configuration separate from your operations and further allows you to have a consistent configuration across multiple servers using variables and conditional logic (such as if statements) to vary only the parts of configuration that need to differ per host, group, or region. Taking a very simple example, assume on our index.html home page we would like to insert the name of the host that has served the page. This is a great first step, as it can help later to determine if a load balancer is working as expected.

Before getting into the nitty-gritty of the template itself, we should familiarize ourselves with the `template` module. As with all tasks in ansible, templates are just another module that we execute from the playbook. As always, it is documented well both via `ansible-doc` and on the Ansible documentation website. In fact, when creating the `webservers.yml` playbook, we used a module named `copy` to copy the `index.html` home page from the local ansible controller to the web servers. We passed the `copy` module attributes called `src` for the source filename and `dest` for the destination filename. This module looked for the source file in a directory relative to the Ansible playbook named `files` – which we created.

The `template` module is very similar to the copy module; however, before copying the file to the remote host, the `template` module will pass the source file through Jinja2 to be processed by the templating engine – meaning we can add variables and control structure directly into our source file. Similar to the `copy` module, which expects to find source files in a directory named files, the `template` module expects to find source files in a directory named `templates`.

Templating index.html

In your Ansible working directory on the controller, create a new directory named templates using the `mkdir` command:

```
mkdir templates
```

Create a new file named `templates/index.html.j2`:

```
My website, served from {{ inventory_hostname }}
```

Note   We add a .j2 suffix to the end of the filename to signify that this is a Jinja2 file. It is not a requirement, just best practice.

Notice that the Jinja2 variable is right there inside the template. Because the template will be parsed by Jinja2 before being copied to the server, we can use all features that Jinja2 provides inside the template.

Now in the `webservers.yml` playbook, replace the original `copy` task for index.html with the new `template` task, such that

```
- name: Push website content to the web root
  copy:
    src: index.html
    dest: /var/www/html/
    mode: u=rw,g=r,o=r
```

is replaced with

```
- name: Push website content to the web root
  template:
    src: index.html.j2
    dest: /var/www/html/index.html
    mode: u=rw,g=r,o=r
```

That's it. You have created your first template, and it doesn't feel all that different to anything else we have done with Ansible. Let's run the playbook to see what happens:

```
> ansible-playbook webservers.yml

PLAY [webservers] ****

TASK [Gathering Facts] ****
ok: [web-002.local]
ok: [web-001.local]

TASK [Ensure nginx is installed] ****
ok: [web-002.local]
ok: [web-001.local]

TASK [Change the nginx port] ****
ok: [web-002.local]
ok: [web-001.local]

TASK [Ensure nginx status is enabled] ****
ok: [web-002.local]
ok: [web-001.local]

TASK [Reload nginx for new config] ****
changed: [web-002.local]
changed: [web-001.local]

TASK [Push website content to the web root] ****
changed: [web-002.local]
changed: [web-001.local]

<truncated>
```

The task to push website content to the web root made a change. That is because the new content differs from the original content that was already on the web servers. The `template` module, as with other Ansible modules, is *idempotent*, meaning if we ran the same playbook again, the module would not make further changes.

To see this change in action, you need to visit both of the webservers via your web browser and observe the difference:

`http://web-001.local:8080/` or `http://192.168.98.111:8080/`

and

`http://web-002.local:8080/` or `http://192.168.98.112:8080/`

The website shown for each should now include the hostname of the web server that served the page – all from a single template file on the Ansible controller, using Jinja2 variables.

Templating Configuration Files

Another practical use of templates is creating configuration files with dynamic content, whether they are pushed to a single host or 1000s – templating brings flexibility and readability to your playbooks. Consider how nginx is currently being configured, task by task using modules such as `replace`, `lineinfile`, and `blockinfile`. Over time, those playbooks become huge and unwieldy; understanding the configuration that will end up on your web servers is almost impossible and not a good use of our precious time.

A much more elegant way of expressing your configuration files in Ansible and pushing them to your hosts is via templating.

To achieve this, we do not modify the core `nginx.conf` file either directly or using Ansible modules, but instead leverage the power of snippets by modifying the `sites-enabled/default` file within the nginx configuration directory. Snippets or include files enable one to drop in additional configuration files that are included by the main file. This is a perfect fit for configuration management tools, such as Ansible, that need to dynamically modify configurations.

If you are not familiar with nginx configuration structure, that is ok – we will walk through it together.

Create a new file, templates/nginx-default.j2:

```
server {
  listen {{ http_port }} default_server;

  root /var/www/html;

  server_name _;

  location /{{ status_url | default('status') }} {
    stub_status on;
  }
}
```

Now open webservers.yml and **delete** the following tasks:

```
- name: Ensure nginx status is enabled
  blockinfile:
    path: /etc/nginx/sites-enabled/default
    insertafter: "^server {"
    block: |
     location /{{ status_url | default('status') }} {
       stub_status on;
     }

- name: Change the nginx port
  replace:
    path: /etc/nginx/sites-enabled/default
    regexp: "listen [0-9]+"
    replace: "listen {{ http_port }}"
```

155

In their place, *before* the task to `Reload nginx for new config`, **add** the following task in bold:

```
- name: Ensure nginx is installed
  apt:
    name: nginx
    state: present
```

```
- name: Configure nginx
  template:
    src: nginx-default.j2
    dest: /etc/nginx/sites-available/default
    mode: u=rw,g=r,o=r
```

```
- name: Reload nginx for new config
  service:
    name: nginx
    state: reloaded
```

That should ensure that the nginx configuration template is rendered on the ansible controller, before being pushed to the web servers. The unsightly tasks have been replaced by a single template task and a clear configuration file that resembles the final configuration as it will be on the remote hosts, albeit with some important variables. Let's run this playbook now:

```
> ansible-playbook webservers.yml

PLAY [webservers] ****

TASK [Gathering Facts] ****
ok: [web-002.local]
ok: [web-001.local]
```

```
TASK [Ensure nginx is installed] ****
ok: [web-002.local]
ok: [web-001.local]
```

TASK [Configure nginx] **
changed: [web-002.local]
changed: [web-001.local]**

TASK [Reload nginx for new config] **
changed: [web-002.local]
changed: [web-001.local]**

The new configuration was pushed by the new `Configure nginx` task, and nginx was reloaded to pick up the new configuration. Now we must confirm that nginx is indeed still serving our content:

http://web-001.local:8080/ or http://192.168.98.111:8080/

and

http://web-002.local:8080/ or http://192.168.98.112:8080/

It is worth understanding how that templated file was rendered and pushed to the remote host. We can do that by connecting to the remote host manually and looking at the file. That can be achieved with a single command on the ansible controller:

```
> ssh web-001.local cat /etc/nginx/sites-available/default

server {
        listen 8080 default_server;

        root /var/www/html;

        server_name _;

        location /status {
```

```
        stub_status on;
    }
}
```

As you can see, variables were replaced with their respective values, and the default( ) filter was used to automatically complete the status page location.

Controlling Flow

Perhaps, there is a reason we have not defined the `status_url`. It could be simply that we forgot and therefore have a sensible default. But what if the expectation was that **if** the `status_url` was not set, then it **should not** be enabled at all? That is often the case for security reasons where a web server is public facing, such that you don't leak internal state information to the outside world.

Conditionals

To achieve that, we would need to replace our default filter applied to the `status_url` to something else – a *conditional*. A conditional is something that will only run a specific branch of code on condition that a specific test passes. The most common application of this is using an **if** statement to determine if statement is true, then perform an action, otherwise do nothing.

Open `templates/nginx-default.j2` and add a conditional check for `status_url` being defined before adding it:

```
server {
  listen {{ http_port }} default_server;

  root /var/www/html;
```

```
server_name _;

    {% if status_url is defined -%}
    location /{{ status_url }} {
        stub_status on;
    }
    {%- endif %}

}
```

There is a magical new incantation, like Jinja2's print statement, but slightly different: {% ... %}. These special characters tell Jinja2 that it should process what is inside as a *statement*, in this case an *if* statement. Variables can be referred to inside statements, and they do not require the usual escape sequence {{ }} as the statement is already being processed by Jinja2 – as is the case here with status_url. Jinja2 statements are processed using Python, so there will be a lot of similarity here – for example, is defined is a special way to say the variable has been set with a value. You may remember the Ansible error earlier when we first added status_url, complaining that the variable was undefined. That is exactly the state that this statement is checking for.

Finally, we must end the if statement. All of the content between the start of the statement {% if ... %} and the end of the statement {% endif %} will only be printed, or included in the resulting file, **if** the statement is true.

Note   You may notice in this example that there are hyphens before and after the statement escape sequences. Those are for whitespace control, which we will cover briefly later.

To see this in action, add a host variable for status_url to web-002. local in the inventory file. Open inventory/webservers:

```
---
webservers:
  hosts:
    web-001.local:
    web-002.local:
    status_url: "status"
```

The expectation would be that web-001.local would not have the status page configured, while web-002.local would – all from a single template file. Let's run the playbook and see:

```
> ansible-playbook webservers.yml

> ssh web-001.local cat /etc/nginx/sites-available/default

server {
    listen 8080 default_server;

    root /var/www/html;

    server_name _;

}

> ssh web-002.local cat /etc/nginx/sites-available/default
server {
    listen 8080 default_server;

    root /var/www/html;

    server_name _;

    location /status {
```

```
        stub_status on;
    }
}
```

Only web-002.local has the status page configured as expected. web-001.local does not have it, as the status_url variable was not defined for web-001.local.

Hint   If you start to notice your configurations are diverging so much that you require dozens of conditionals, it might be time to split it up into two or more different templates, making use of include files that are available in most applications today.

Loops

Along with if statements, we can use another type of flow control – the for loop. The for loop allows you to loop over a list or dictionary (such as those in ansible_facts) and perform an action for each item in the list or dictionary. This can be useful for generating configuration files from a list, such as for firewall rules, or perhaps a load balancer that needs to have a block of configuration per backend web server that it supports, something we will build later.

For now, we will provide some more detailed information from ansible_facts via the website content to show off how you might use a for loop in an Ansible template.

Open templates/index.html.j2 and add a new for loop:

```
My website, served from {{ inventory_hostname }}
```

```
<p>
IP Addresses:<br />
{% for ip in ansible_all_ipv4_addresses %}
    {{ ip }}<br />
{% endfor %}
</p>
```

Here, we are asking Jinja2 to loop over each element in the ansible fact named ansible_all_ipv4_addresses, which is a list, and for each iteration of the for loop, assign the current value from the list to the variable named ip. We then use that variable as a normal Jinja2 variable inside the content of the for loop before ending the loop in the same way we previously ended the if statement.

Let's run the playbook again and see the results:

```
> ansible-playbook webservers.yml
```

Now visit each of the web servers via your web browser and see that the ansible fact for ansible_all_ipv4_addresses has now become part of the web page content. To understand what this template resolves to, you can use SSH again to display the contents of the file:

http://web-001.local:8080/ or http://192.168.98.111:8080/

and

http://web-002.local:8080/ or http://192.168.98.112:8080/

```
> ssh web-001.local cat /var/www/html/index.html
```

My website, served from web-001.local

```
<p>
IP Addresses:<br />
    10.0.2.15<br />
    192.168.98.111<br />
</p>
```

This is the simplest form of a for loop, looping over a list of elements. When working with dictionaries, it is worth noting that some additional work is required, since dictionary items are actually key-value pairs themselves, not just simple elements.

Let's quickly add a new for loop, this time using a dictionary:

```
My website, served from {{ inventory_hostname }}

<p>
IP Addresses:<br />
{% for ip in ansible_all_ipv4_addresses %}
    {{ ip }}<br />
{% endfor %}
</p>

<p>
Operating System:<br />
{% for key, value in ansible_lsb.items() %}
    {{ key }}: {{ value }}<br />
{% endfor %}
</p>
```

Now we have two variables to assign the elements to, rather than one – that is because a dictionary item consists of a key and a value. Let's look at ansible_lsb to understand this better:

```
> ansible -m setup -a 'filter=ansible_lsb' web-001.local

web-001.local | SUCCESS => {
    "ansible_facts": {
        "ansible_lsb": {
            "codename": "focal",
            "description": "Ubuntu 20.04.1 LTS",
            "id": "Ubuntu",
```

```
        "major_release": "20",
        "release": "20.04"
    },
    "discovered_interpreter_python": "/usr/bin/python3"
},
"changed": false
}
```

Notice the key-value pairs such as codename: focal. In the for loop, the first variable aptly named key would be assigned the element to the left, the key (codename). The second variable in the for loop would be assigned the element to the right, the value (focal).

The suffix .items() is a special function to ensure two values, the key and the value, are passed to the for loop.

Let's run this playbook and see the results:

```
> ansible-playbook webservers.yml

> ssh web-001.local cat /var/www/html/index.html

My website, served from web-001.local

<p>
IP Addresses:<br />
    10.0.2.15<br />
    192.168.98.111<br />
</p>

<p>
IP Addresses:<br />
    id: Ubuntu<br />
    description: Ubuntu 20.04.3 LTS<br />
    release: 20.04<br />
```

```
      codename: focal<br />
      major_release: 20<br />
</p>
```

Whitespace

By default, Jinja2 takes a number of actions relating to whitespace in your templates – which can really catch you out if the resulting file requires strict control over whitespace, such as some configuration file formats that depend on indentation.

Because of this, it is important to understand what Jinja2 is doing with whitespace and how you can manipulate it to get the results you are looking for. This has caught many people out, many times, and at times can be infuriating to get right. Here is a short summary, but the key is to play around with it and see what happens.

Whitespace is defined as

1. Spaces

2. Tabs

3. Newlines

When using statements in Jinja2, whitespace surrounding the start and end of the statement is not touched by default; however, Ansible version 2.4 and above change that configuration to ensure that newlines at the end of an expression line are automatically removed.

Take, for example

```
<div>
    {% if say_hello %}
      Hello, world
    {% endif %}
</div>
```

The whitespace (including newline) at the end of those statements will be automatically removed by Jinja2; however, the whitespace **before** the statement will not. Therefore, the whitespace (spaces) before the if statement would actually contribute toward your content, referred to by the following asterisks for clarity:

```
<div>
****    Hello, world
****</div>
```

The asterisks represent whitespace that has been added because of the whitespace **before** the statement in the template. As the newline at the end of the statement is automatically removed, that indentation whitespace is applied to the following line; in this case, the Hello, world text and the </div> line have additional indentation. To visualize this, see the template again but with the same asterisks added:

```
<div>
****{% if say_hello %}
    Hello, world
****{% endif %}
</div>
```

To fix this, we can instruct Jinja2 to remove whitespace before and after the statements, as needed, by appending a minus sign directly adjacent to the % character. In this case, we would want to remove the whitespace before the statement, right? *Reminder: Newlines are considered whitespace, making this a bad idea.*

```
<div>
    {%- if say_hello %}
      Hello, world
      {%- endif %}
</div>
```

That will remove the newlines and space before the statement, meaning the newline after `<div>` and the newline after the word `world` would be removed, resulting in

```
<div>    Hello, world</div>
```

This is a difficult situation indeed. The combination of Ansible removing newlines at the end of the statement by default actually makes it quite difficult to achieve what we are looking for. The most sensible option to preserve your sanity would simply be to not indent the Jinja2 statements at all:

```
<div>
{% if say_hello %}
    Hello, world
{% endif %}
</div>
```

Resulting in the correct formatting:

```
<div>
    Hello, world
</div>
```

Summary

Jinja2 and templates are powerful, but are also a lot to take in. The key is to keep it simple and build up your templates carefully – understanding what needs to be dynamic and what needs to be static.

In our experience, filters are one of the most used features of Jinja2. Remember that an Ansible variable is parsed using Jinja2, so filters can also be placed right inside your playbooks. They can manipulate data in many ways, and there are dozens of filters available – we find ourselves checking the documentation even today to familiarize ourselves with the best filter choice for the occasion. There are filters to modify text, to perform arithmetic on sets of numbers, to select a value from many at random, or even to search through dictionaries, returning only elements that match a specific string (useful for things like `ansible_mounts`). Filters provide a lot of the power for Jinja2.

We showed how one particular filter can be used in our playbooks to define the default value a variable will take if it has not been otherwise defined. That can be especially useful when working with elements that have a clear default value such as `http_port` defaulting to port 80.

We then brought these concepts together to create a template for our web page content, allowing us to incorporate variables into an otherwise static content page and bringing our nginx configuration file into our Ansible playbooks while making use of dynamic variables such as the HTTP port and conditionals to determine whether or not to enable the special status URL.

We then looked at some simple `for` loops allowing us to iterate over some data in the form of Ansible facts and include even more dynamic content to our web page in the form of IP addresses and operating system information. One key benefit of this pattern is that as we add more IP addresses to the host, we never need touch the template again – those IP addresses will automatically be pulled into the rendered template every time the playbook is run.

Finally, we explored whitespace, a tricky subject in Jinja2 that can easily catch you out in weird and wonderful ways. There are clear rules to how whitespace is managed, but it isn't always intuitive – so you may need to think about this. For the most part, it won't matter all that much, but for configuration files that rely on specific indentation or formatting, you should be aware of how whitespace is handled.

This gives a brief introduction into a diverse topic. Jinja2 is simple, yet so powerful. It could fill a book in its own right, so we strongly urge you to search online and learn more about Jinja2 through practical experience.

CHAPTER 8

Handling Change

Everything changes. Nothing is more true than when managing your infrastructure which is often in a constant state of flux. Configuration files, content, and application versions are changing all the time. That means we need a way of handling changes when they happen and leaving things well alone at other times so as not to break things that currently work well. This is the core tenet of idempotence.

Consider your messaging app on your mobile phone. How much time and effort would you waste if you were forced to check inside the messaging app every time you picked up your phone to determine if new messages required your attention? How much would that interrupt the service that is your life? A lot! That is why we have notifications. Usually, a small red blob with a number inside is shown on the messaging app's icon which is designed to *notify* us that something has changed. Regardless of the number of messages you have received, only one notification is needed to know that the app requires your attention. In reality, messages are unique, and we would receive one notification per message – but regardless of the number of messages, we would only need to open the app once to read them all.

Wouldn't it be really useful if we could do the same for our services with our Ansible playbooks? Well, we're in luck! Ansible has just that in the form of *handlers* – a specific type of task designed to *handle notifications*.

You may have noticed that we have previously handled changes to our nginx configuration with two specific tasks: one to *push the configuration*

© Shaun R Smith and Peter Membrey 2022
S. R. Smith and P. Membrey, *Beginning Ansible Concepts and Application*,
https://doi.org/10.1007/978-1-4842-8173-4_8

file and the second to *restart nginx*. That task, restarting nginx, by its very nature is **not** idempotent – it always restarts nginx. In the real world, we would not want nginx to restart every single time we run our Ansible playbook, as it is a service-impacting action (think: temporary service outage). If nothing has changed, why create an unnecessary blip for our users? We should only restart or reload configuration when the configuration has actually changed.

What Is a Handler?

Despite having a different name and a different place to live within your Ansible playbook directory structure, a handler is nothing more than another *task*. By that definition, a handler can do anything a task can do; it can call any module with any combination of attributes.

However, contrary to a normal task, a handler will not run as part of your playbook. The handler is run **if and only if** it has been *notified* directly of a change by another task within your playbook. Similar to how there isn't much point in opening your messaging app unless you have a notification. It is a specific form of conditional logic that depends on input from other tasks.

Writing Your Handler

We will work with the simple nginx configuration again from Chapter 7. If you do not already have that configuration to hand, please download the source code and find it in the directory named chapter08.

Open the playbook webservers.yml and ensure the content is as follows. If you are jumping in here, then you will need the entire file content; otherwise, focus on the additions in bold:

```
---
- hosts: webservers
  become: true
  handlers:
    - name: Reload nginx
      service:
        name: nginx
        state: reloaded
  tasks:
    - name: Ensure nginx is installed
      apt:
        name: nginx
        state: present

    - name: Configure nginx
      template:
        src: nginx-default.j2
        dest: /etc/nginx/sites-available/default

    - name: Reload nginx for new config
      service:
        name: nginx
        state: reloaded

    - name: Push website content to the web root
      template:
        src: index.html.j2
        dest: /var/www/html/index.html

    - name: Firewall - Allow SSH connections
      ufw:
        rule: allow
        name: OpenSSH
```

```
- name: Firewall - Allow website connections
  ufw:
    rule: allow
    port: "{{ http_port }}"

- name: Firewall - Deny everything else
  ufw:
    state: enabled
    policy: deny

- name: Validate that the http_port is working
  wait_for:
    host: "{{ ansible_host }}"
    port: "{{ http_port }}"
    timeout: 5
  connection: local
```

As mentioned, handlers are simply a task defined in a different location within the playbook. In this case, they are under a heading of *handlers*, rather than *tasks* – which tells Ansible to treat them differently.

Running this playbook, we can see that the handler that we just added is *inert*, meaning it does **not** get run:

```
> ansible-playbook webservers.yml

PLAY [webservers] ****

TASK [Gathering Facts] ****
ok: [web-001.local]
ok: [web-002.local]

TASK [Ensure nginx is installed] ****
ok: [web-001.local]
ok: [web-002.local]
```

```
TASK [Configure nginx] ****
ok: [web-001.local]
ok: [web-002.local]

TASK [Reload nginx for new config] ****
changed: [web-002.local]
changed: [web-001.local]

TASK [Push website content to the web root] ****
ok: [web-001.local]
ok: [web-002.local]

TASK [Firewall - Allow SSH connections] ****
ok: [web-001.local]
ok: [web-002.local]

TASK [Firewall - Allow website connections] ****
ok: [web-001.local]
ok: [web-002.local]

TASK [Firewall - Deny everything else] ****
ok: [web-001.local]
ok: [web-002.local]

TASK [Validate that the http_port is working] ****
ok: [web-002.local]
ok: [web-001.local]
```

Looking through the preceding output, the new handler named "*Reload nginx*" was not run at all. We can however notice that the original task "*Reload nginx for new config*" is marked changed, exhibiting the very problem we discussed at the start of this chapter – that this playbook will **always** reload nginx despite configuration not changing.

But what about the handler we added? It didn't do anything. While we added the handler, we didn't yet notify it of changes and so it did not run. It doesn't know it is supposed to. Let's modify the playbook once again, this time **removing** the original "*Reload nginx for new config*" task and **adding** a notification for the new "*Reload nginx*" handler:

```
---
- hosts: webservers
  become: true
  handlers:
    - name: Reload nginx
      service:
        name: nginx
        state: reloaded
  tasks:
    - name: Ensure nginx is installed
      apt:
        name: nginx
        state: present

    - name: Configure nginx
      template:
        src: nginx-default.j2
        dest: /etc/nginx/sites-available/default
      notify: "Reload nginx"

[DELETE]
    - name: Reload nginx for new config
      service:
        name: nginx
        state: reloaded

    - name: Push website content to the web root
      template:
```

```
src: index.html.j2
dest: /var/www/html/index.html
```

[truncated to reduce space in the book]

Important   Pay attention to indentation when writing your playbooks. The notify keyword is in line with the module name; it is an attribute of the task, not of the module itself.

Let's run that playbook again:

```
> ansible-playbook webservers.yml

PLAY [webservers] ****

TASK [Gathering Facts] ****
ok: [web-002.local]
ok: [web-001.local]

TASK [Ensure nginx is installed] ****
ok: [web-002.local]
ok: [web-001.local]

TASK [Configure nginx] ****
ok: [web-001.local]
ok: [web-002.local]

TASK [Push website content to the web root] ****
ok: [web-001.local]
ok: [web-002.local]

TASK [Firewall - Allow SSH connections] ****
ok: [web-002.local]
ok: [web-001.local]
```

```
TASK [Firewall - Allow website connections] ****
ok: [web-001.local]
ok: [web-002.local]

TASK [Firewall - Deny everything else] ****
ok: [web-002.local]
ok: [web-001.local]

TASK [Validate that the http_port is working] ****
ok: [web-002.local]
ok: [web-001.local]
```

Still no sign of the new handler running. What went wrong? Nothing at all. The task that is set to notify the handler *"Configure nginx"* shows an *ok* state for both web server hosts, meaning it was not changed.

This is an important observation – the handler is not notified unless it is needed. Ansible determines notification being needed **if and only if** the task has made a *change* to the host in which case the status would show *changed* (remember that changed: true/false in verbose mode earlier in the book?). In this case, the task doing the notifying is "Configure nginx," and it did not change.

Let's modify our configuration template and see the handler in action. Open up the configuration file templates/nginx-default.j2 and add a comment line:

```
# The default server configuration
server {
        listen {{ http_port }} default_server;

        root /var/www/html;

        server_name _;

        {% if status_url is defined -%}
        location /{{ status_url }} {
```

```
        stub_status on;
    }
    {%- endif %}

}
```

Once that is done, run the playbook once more:

```
> ansible-playbook webservers.yml

PLAY [webservers] ****

TASK [Gathering Facts] ****
ok: [web-001.local]
ok: [web-002.local]

TASK [Ensure nginx is installed] ****
ok: [web-001.local]
ok: [web-002.local]

TASK [Configure nginx] ****
changed: [web-002.local]
changed: [web-001.local]

TASK [Push website content to the web root] ****
ok: [web-002.local]
ok: [web-001.local]

TASK [Firewall - Allow SSH connections] ****
ok: [web-001.local]
ok: [web-002.local]

TASK [Firewall - Allow website connections] ****
ok: [web-002.local]
ok: [web-001.local]

TASK [Firewall - Deny everything else] ****
```

```
ok: [web-001.local]
ok: [web-002.local]

TASK [Validate that the http_port is working] ****
ok: [web-001.local]
ok: [web-002.local]
```

RUNNING HANDLER [Reload nginx] ****
changed: [web-002.local]
changed: [web-001.local]

This time, the configuration task "*Configure nginx*" reported that it had made a change to both webserver hosts (web-001 and web-002), and at the end of the playbook run, there is a new message "RUNNING HANDLER," followed by the "*Reload nginx*" handler that we wrote earlier running against both hosts.

Handlers Run Only Once

It is important to note that a handler can be notified any number of times throughout the playbook. Perhaps, there are numerous tasks that justify running a handler, such as upgrading packages, adding modules, changing configuration, modifying content, restarting backend services, etc. - all these tasks can notify the *same* handler. Ansible manages these notifications such that the handler will only run once at the end of the play. This ensures the least interruption necessary to any running services.

Handlers Run at the End, Usually

Another thing to notice in the preceding playbook execution is the task to validate that the http_port is working executed *before* the handler to Reload nginx. That happens to be ok in this particular run, since nginx was already configured during a previous run and therefore was already listening on the correct port; however, that is unlikely to always be the case. If we were running Ansible against a new host, it would fail on the *"Validate that the http_port is working"* task, because nginx has not yet been restarted to pick up its new configuration.

This ordering is important. Handlers usually run at the end of a block of tasks. Currently, this is at the end of the play (remember a playbook can contain multiple plays), but later when we start looking into roles, we will see that a "block of tasks" can be split into a number of playbook concepts such as pre_tasks, roles, and post_tasks. At the end of each block of tasks, handlers for that section are run.

Handlers always run in the order that they have been defined in your playbook files, and not in the order that they are notified. This is important if you have multiple handlers that must run in a specific order, as you must write them in that order – it makes no difference in what order you notify them. This is useful when notifying handlers from many different places within a structured playbook, as you do not need to worry about reordering your playbook flow to accommodate handler ordering.

You can break out of this and force handlers to run any time within your playbook by "flushing" them. This can be useful if you know handlers must run before continuing to the next set of tasks, and it can appear anywhere within your playbook. It is triggered using a new keyword, meta:

```
---
- hosts: webservers
  become: true
  handlers:
    - name: Reload nginx
      service:
        name: nginx
        state: reloaded
  tasks:
    - name: Ensure nginx is installed
```

```
  apt:
    name: nginx
    state: present

- name: Configure nginx
  template:
    src: nginx-default.j2
    dest: /etc/nginx/sites-available/default
  notify: "Reload nginx"

- meta: flush_handlers
```

The "*Reload nginx*" handler will now be run immediately following the "*Configure nginx*" task and will no longer run at the end of the group of tasks as it previously did. Importantly, before the http_port validation task:

```
> ansible-playbook webservers.yml

PLAY [webservers] ****

TASK [Gathering Facts] ****
ok: [web-001.local]
ok: [web-002.local]

TASK [Ensure nginx is installed] ****
ok: [web-002.local]
ok: [web-001.local]

TASK [Configure nginx] ****
changed: [web-002.local]
changed: [web-001.local]

RUNNING HANDLER [Reload nginx] ****
changed: [web-002.local]
changed: [web-001.local]
```

```
TASK [Push website content to the web root] ****
ok: [web-001.local]
ok: [web-002.local]

TASK [Firewall - Allow SSH connections] ****
ok: [web-002.local]
ok: [web-001.local]

TASK [Firewall - Allow website connections] ****
ok: [web-001.local]
ok: [web-002.local]

TASK [Firewall - Deny everything else] ****
ok: [web-001.local]
ok: [web-002.local]

TASK [Validate that the http_port is working] ****
ok: [web-001.local]
ok: [web-002.local]
```

Grouping Handlers with listen

While that indeed works, having flush_handlers all over your playbooks will quickly become confusing and somewhat defeats the purpose. A better option might be to also make the http_port validation a handler, which is also triggered when making a change to the nginx configuration. However, a task can only notify a single handler.

Sometimes, it would be useful to group handlers together and notify them together. Imagine that when you are making a change to your application service, you also want to reload the frontend web server; or when reloading your database service, you must also reload the consumer of that service such that it reconnects smoothly. That is difficult with raw handlers.

To this end, Ansible supports a concept known as "subscribing" the handler to a *notification topic* and having your task notify the *topic* of a change, rather than notifying the handler directly. Think of this as subscribing to a digital TV package – you choose the entertainment package and as a result can watch any number of additional TV channels, yet your bill simply shows you the *topic* that you have subscribed to, entertainment; and many other people may subscribe to that same topic and receive the same channels. So it is with notification topics and handlers – many handlers subscribe to a topic, and you notify the topic on change. The result is that all subscribed handlers will run at the corresponding time once the topic has been notified of a change.

One thing to keep in mind is that you don't have to strictly define your topic. The fact that it is listened to/notified means it implicitly exists; there is no magic incantation to bring it into existence. This makes it incredibly easy to use by simply telling the handler to listen for notifications on that topic, in *addition* to the usual direct notifications we saw earlier.

Let's modify our handler to use a notification topic and remove the *flush_handlers* task that we added in the previous step. We will also migrate the http_port validation task to be a handler and subscribe it to the *same* notification topic:

```
---
- hosts: webservers
  become: true
  handlers:
    - name: Reload nginx
      service:
        name: nginx
        state: reloaded
      listen: "Reload web services"

    - name: Validate that the http_port is working
      wait_for:
```

```
      host: "{{ ansible_host }}"
      port: "{{ http_port }}"
      timeout: 5
    connection: local
    listen: "Reload web services"
tasks:
- name: Ensure nginx is installed
  apt:
    name: nginx
    state: present

- name: Configure nginx
  template:
    src: nginx-default.j2
    dest: /etc/nginx/sites-available/default
    force: yes
  notify: "Reload web services"

- name: Push website content to the web root
  template:
    src: index.html.j2
    dest: /var/www/html/index.html

- name: Firewall - Allow SSH connections
  ufw:
    rule: allow
    name: OpenSSH

- name: Firewall - Allow website connections
  ufw:
    rule: allow
    port: "{{ http_port }}"
```

```
- name: Firewall - Deny everything else
  ufw:
    state: enabled
    policy: deny
```

Now, modify the template/nginx-default.j2 file and remove the comment line we had previously added. The line's content isn't important; we are just ensuring the configuration file in Ansible is different to what is on the server to trigger a "change." Then run the playbook:

```
> ansible-playbook webservers.yml

PLAY [webservers] ****

TASK [Gathering Facts] ****
ok: [web-002.local]
ok: [web-001.local]

TASK [Ensure nginx is installed] ****
ok: [web-002.local]
ok: [web-001.local]

TASK [Configure nginx] ****
changed: [web-001.local]
changed: [web-002.local]

TASK [Push website content to the web root] ****
ok: [web-002.local]
ok: [web-001.local]

TASK [Firewall - Allow SSH connections] ****
ok: [web-002.local]
ok: [web-001.local]

TASK [Firewall - Allow website connections] ****
ok: [web-001.local]
ok: [web-002.local]
```

```
TASK [Firewall - Deny everything else] ****
ok: [web-002.local]
ok: [web-001.local]
```

RUNNING HANDLER [Reload nginx] ****
changed: [web-002.local]
changed: [web-001.local]

RUNNING HANDLER [Validate that the http_port is working] ****
ok: [web-002.local]
ok: [web-001.local]

The handlers both ran, based this time on being subscribed to the same notification topic "*Reload web services*." We might have many handlers all subscribed to this notification topic – and on being notified, *all* handlers subscribed to that topic would be notified to run. This is a great way of managing complex interactions when reloading services.

It is also important to note that the handlers ran in the order that they were written in the playbook. It makes no difference how or when they are notified, they will *always* run in the order defined. In this case, that is critical, since we must reload nginx before testing that it is accessible.

Exercise: Modify Your Upgrade Playbook to Only Reboot When a Reboot Is Required

The simple approach to rebooting on package upgrade would be to use a handler which simply issues the reboot when the upgrade packages task has completed, and that may serve you perfectly well during testing, but may result in some wasted time. Not all package upgrades on a Debian/Ubuntu system will require a reboot; in fact, few will. To help with this, when a reboot is likely to be required, a file is created named */var/run/ reboot-required*.

Modify the upgrade.yml playbook to take this into account.

We are using automatic reboot as an example to gain familiarity with Ansible concepts. In a production environment, you would almost never want to simply reboot a host because a package update says a reboot is needed. You will want to consider a number of factors including maintenance windows, automatic failover, etc.

CHAPTER 9

Roles: Ansible's Packing Cubes

Throughout the book, we have been building up our playbook in a manner akin to grabbing a suitcase and just tossing in all of our clothes, toiletries, and accessories wherever they may fit. That is currently fine as we have only defined a single use case to this point, web servers, but even there we are performing increasingly more ordered tasks with the risk of losing control.

If you've never used them, we highly recommend grabbing yourself some packing cubes before your next holiday – they allow you to bring order to the chaos that is your suitcase packing. You add all items of a particular type (be it clothing, toiletries, jewelry, electronic devices, batteries, etc.) to one or more packing cubes, which close and can be packed independently. Doing so keeps the main compartment of your suitcase clean and tidy and enables you to instantly jump to only the relevant cube you need to achieve your current task – be it getting dressed, charging batteries, or taking a shower. Simply open up the relevant cube and off you go.

Just like with our suitcase packing, our Ansible playbooks can benefit from some order among the chaos. For that, we have virtual packing cubes, or as Ansible calls them: *roles*.

© Shaun R Smith and Peter Membrey 2022
S. R. Smith and P. Membrey, *Beginning Ansible Concepts and Application*,
https://doi.org/10.1007/978-1-4842-8173-4_9

Roles are all the above, and much more. They enable the idea of reusable code within Ansible. They group functionality that achieves a particular set of tasks into an independent *packing cube* which can be dropped into your Ansible playbooks and used time and again across many other playbooks. Some examples may be a role to safely upgrade system packages, to set up a basic firewall, SSH access to a server, or to install and configure a simple secure web server. This concept of reusability may or may not be true, depending on how you slice and dice your roles – for many of our projects, it is not practical or necessary (as it may add additional fragmentation of our code for little benefit), but it is always possible.

A practical example might be configuring a firewall. One could define a single role per firewall rule grouping such as "Allow web server inbound," "Allow web requests outbound," etc. But doing so adds a lot of overhead for little gain. The practical solution would be to simply have a base firewall role that sets up a default drop policy while allowing SSH access in, alongside a domain-specific firewall role for the project in question. This provides reusable core components, without taking it to an impractical and difficult-to-maintain extreme.

With that said, let's explore Ansible roles.

What's in a Role?

We defined a role as "*a grouping of functionality to achieve a particular set of tasks.*" A role at its core is a directory structure, which starts at the top level with the role name and below that a directory per component that contributes to the role's function. The role's functionality follows that of Ansible itself – a role may contain many features of Ansible that you have already been learning throughout this book, including

1. Tasks – Just like our playbooks

2. Handlers – Just like our playbooks

3. Variables – Both defaults and overrides

4. Files and templates (as used by copy and template modules)

5. Dependencies

6. Custom modules

All of these are grouped into directories beneath the role itself, meaning that the role is an isolated grouping of code that can achieve a particular outcome. Because it contains everything needed to achieve the desired result, we can drop this role into a different Ansible playbook and achieve the same outcome, without reinventing the wheel. That is why we often consider roles to be reusable code.

Walk-Through: Web Server Installation

The easiest way to learn how to structure a role is through experience. This may appear tricky at first, but by the end it should all make perfect sense and make you want to use roles more.

First, start by creating the directory structure for the new roles. So far, our playbook performs two distinct actions:

1. Install and configure the web server

2. Set up the firewall rules, one of which is the webserver rule

We have two options to address the firewall rules, both of which come with their own challenges:

1. A single role named firewall, with all firewall rules included. This has the advantage of keeping the firewall configuration in one place, with the downside of needing to manage the web server setup (HTTP port, firewall) across two separate roles.

2. A common role named firewall, for the server-
    specific configuration such as SSH access, with the
    webserver-specific firewall rule in the webserver
    roles alongside the service that it is allowing through.
    The downside to this is the role is tied to the specific
    firewall application used in the codebase.

For the purpose of managing this specific codebase, we will opt for
option 2 as it simplifies the setting of variables and managing of services.
If you opted to create truly reusable roles for use across multiple operating
systems, you may decide differently, but Ansible is flexible enough to
provide both.

On the ansible controller, ensure you are in the correct directory and
create two new roles:

```
cd /vagrant
```

```
mkdir -p roles/webserver/tasks/
mkdir -p roles/webserver/templates/
```

```
mkdir -p roles/firewall/tasks/
```

Passing -p to the mkdir command instructs it to create all *parent*
directories needed. In this case, the roles/, roles/webserver/, and then
roles/webserver/tasks/ directories will all be created, in that order.

Moving Tasks

Taking the *webservers.yml* playbook from previous chapters, we will need
to move all the tasks from the playbook into a new role, in a specific file
under the *tasks* directory that was just created. We do this by cutting and
pasting all the tasks that appear under the *tasks:* keyword in the original
playbook into a new file.

When including a role, Ansible will always look for the file named *main.yml* inside the various directories, the entry point for executing the tasks from the role being the file *roles/[role name]/tasks/main.yml.*

Remember to move the non-webserver firewall tasks from webservers. yml to the new firewall role and the webserver-related firewall tasks to the webserver role. Go ahead and move those tasks; the resulting files should look like the following:

roles/webserver/tasks/main.yml:

```
- name: Ensure nginx is installed
  apt:
    name: nginx
    state: present

- name: Configure nginx
  template:
    src: nginx-default.j2
    dest: /etc/nginx/sites-available/default
  notify: "Reload web services"

- name: Push website content to the web root
  template:
    src: index.html.j2
    dest: /var/www/html/index.html

- name: Firewall - Allow website connections
  ufw:
    rule: allow
    port: "{{ http_port }}"
```

roles/firewall/tasks/main.yml:

```
- name: Firewall - Allow SSH connections
  ufw:
    rule: allow
    name: OpenSSH

- name: Firewall - Deny everything else
  ufw:
    state: enabled
    policy: deny
```

Migrate the Handler

So far, handlers have been defined inside the main *webservers.yml* playbook alongside the tasks. As we are discussing roles, and modularization, let's talk about how to set our handlers free. As with anything else in Ansible, we can pull out the tasks that act as our handlers into a special location within the role, files live in files/, templates in templates/, and unsurprisingly we put our handlers in a directory named handlers/.

So, from within our webserver/ role, let us create the new directory handlers/ and add a file named main.yml containing our "Reload nginx" handler. We will move the handler from the webservers.yml playbook into this new handlers/main.yml file:

```
> mkdir roles/webserver/handlers/
```

roles/webserver/handlers/main.yml:

```
---
- name: Reload nginx
  service:
    name: nginx
    state: reloaded
  listen: "Reload web services"
```

```
- name: Validate that the http_port is working
  wait_for:
    host: "{{ ansible_host }}"
    port: "{{ http_port }}"
    timeout: 5
  connection: local
  listen: "Reload web services"
```

Migrate Templates

As with the handlers, we should move the webserver-related templates into their respective role, so that they are nicely contained. On the ansible-controller, move the entire templates directory we previously created into this new role:

```
> mv templates/ roles/webserver/
```

Use the New Roles in Your Playbook

For the playbook that has had all its handlers and tasks migrated to roles, we must now add two new tasks which inform Ansible where to find the new roles that we just created and to execute them as part of this playbook. As a result, the final *webservers.yml* file should now look like this:

```
---
- hosts: webservers
  become: true
  tasks:
    - name: Setup firewall
      include_role:
        name: firewall
```

```
- name: Build webservers
  include_role:
    name: webserver
```

Validate Your Structure

The directory structure should now look like this. If it does not, please reread the preceding sections to understand what moved from where – we included the full text of all four files, so if you do need to start over, you can simply create those files manually:

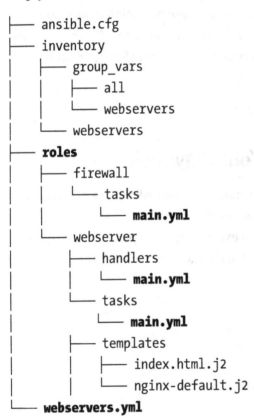

```
├── ansible.cfg
├── inventory
│   ├── group_vars
│   │   ├── all
│   │   └── webservers
│   └── webservers
├── roles
│   ├── firewall
│   │   └── tasks
│   │       └── main.yml
│   └── webserver
│       ├── handlers
│       │   └── main.yml
│       └── tasks
│           └── main.yml
│       ├── templates
│       │   ├── index.html.j2
│       │   └── nginx-default.j2
└── webservers.yml
```

Now we must run the playbook. At this stage, we have changed a lot, including the ordering and structure of the playbook execution, so it makes sense to have a hard reset of the target hosts to ensure our playbook still works as expected. Running against the existing web servers that have already been configured will simply return ok for all of the tasks. Instead, let's destroy and recreate the web server hosts as though they are new servers. To do this, you will need to leave the controller which you can do by logging out and then instructing vagrant to destroy the web-* hosts:

vagrant@ansible-controller$ **logout**

vagrant destroy web-001 web-002

```
    web-002: Are you sure you want to destroy the 'web-002'
    VM? [y/N] y
==> web-002: Forcing shutdown of VM...
==> web-002: Destroying VM and associated drives...
    web-001: Are you sure you want to destroy the 'web-001'
    VM? [y/N] y
==> web-001: Forcing shutdown of VM...
==> web-001: Destroying VM and associated drives...
```

vagrant up web-001 web-002

```
  [lots of output whilst the hosts are configured]
```

When we now run the playbook, we are building two brand-new web servers; hopefully, there is very little difference between this and the previous runs, except now your code is neatly contained in logically arranged packing cubes, or roles:

```
> vagrant ssh controller
> cd /vagrant
> ansible-playbook webservers.yml
```

PLAY [webservers] ****

TASK [Gathering Facts] ****
ok: [web-001.local]
ok: [web-002.local]

TASK [Setup firewall] ****

TASK [**firewall** : Firewall - Allow SSH connections] ****
changed: [web-001.local]
changed: [web-002.local]

TASK [**firewall** : Firewall - Deny everything else] ****
changed: [web-001.local]
changed: [web-002.local]

TASK [Build webservers] ****

TASK [**webserver** : Ensure nginx is installed] ****
ok: [web-002.local]
ok: [web-001.local]

TASK [**webserver** : Configure nginx] ****
changed: [web-002.local]
changed: [web-001.local]

TASK [**webserver** : Push website content to the web root] ****
ok: [web-002.local]
ok: [web-001.local]

TASK [**webserver** : Firewall - Allow website connections] ****
ok: [web-001.local]
ok: [web-002.local]

```
RUNNING HANDLER [webserver : Reload nginx] ****
changed: [web-001.local]
changed: [web-002.local]

RUNNING HANDLER [webserver : Validate that the http_port is
working] ****
ok: [web-001.local]
ok: [web-002.local]
```

First, let us look at the output from the preceding playbook run. It looks slightly different to our previous runs; there is a TASK heading which shows the name we gave to the *include_role* task in the main playbook – this shows as a task, as that is exactly what it is, a task to include a role. Each task that is executed from that role then includes the role name (webserver) as a prefix to the task name, making it noticeably clear which role each task belongs to. This is especially useful for debugging exactly where your playbook has failed as it grows larger.

That means that the website should now be available via the web browser:

```
http://web-001.local:8080/
```

or

```
http://192.168.98.111:8080/
```

Role Structure

To review, the structure of the roles/ directory should now be as described at the start of this chapter, which we can see using the tree command on the ansible-controller:

```
> tree roles

roles/
├── firewall
│   └── tasks
│       └── main.yml
└── webserver
    ├── handlers
    │   └── main.yml
    ├── tasks
    │   └── main.yml
    └── templates
        ├── index.html.j2
        └── nginx-default.j2
```

We can see that tasks, handlers, and templates have all moved into the webserver role, and the firewall role simply has tasks. A role can contain as many or as few of the available features required – it is entirely possible that you have a role that *only* contains a handler, without tasks, for example.

Role Default Variables

The webserver role, as it stands, is quite modular and could easily be reused since it contains most of the code required for execution. The only missing piece of the puzzle is the variable http_port which is used throughout the role. This is currently defined globally using *group_vars* and *host_vars*; however, for a role to be truly reusable, we should not assume the state of the Ansible environment into which the code will be placed. Therefore, we should at the very least provide default values for any variables used within our role, in the role.

Providing a default variable is extremely simple: we create a new directory within the role named *defaults*. Within this directory, as with other directories, place a file named `main.yml` and add your variables alongside their default values for the role:

roles/webserver/defaults/main.yml:

```
---
http_port: 80
```

That is all there is to it. If the *webserver* role is called, and the `http_port` variable is not set, this default value will be applied instead.

Role Dependencies

Some roles you create will have a dependency on another. A great example already exists in our playbook, in that our base firewall configuration should exist before we execute the webserver role, such that our firewall rules are correctly applied. In a small playbook such as ours, this isn't a big deal, since we control the procedural flow. But as playbooks grow, and interdependencies become more complex, we can make our playbooks much more dynamic.

What we really care about is that we set up our web server. It is the webserver that depends on the firewall configuration. Our playbook could just concern itself with the webserver setup. Let the webserver role worry about the fact that it has a dependency on firewall, so we do not need to be so strict on the procedural nature of our playbook.

Let's do that now. We will first remove the firewall `include_role` from our `webservers.yml` playbook, leaving only the webserver role, followed by adding the firewall role as a dependency of the webserver role.

Modify webservers.yml to now look like this:

```
---
- hosts: webservers
  become: true
  tasks:
    - name: Build webservers
      include_role:
        name: webserver
```

We no longer call the firewall role in our playbook. If we were to run this again now, the firewall rules simply would not get created. To ensure the firewall role is called *when needed*, we will add a dependency to the webserver role. To do so, we will create a metadata file in the webserver role directory called *meta*:

```
> mkdir roles/webserver/meta
```

roles/webserver/meta/main.yml:
```
---
dependencies:
  - role: firewall
```

Now, run the playbook again – we should see that the firewall tasks always run *before* the webservers tasks, despite the firewall role not being explicitly called by the playbook. That's because of the dependency we created:

```
> ansible-playbook webservers.yml

PLAY [webservers] ****

TASK [Gathering Facts] ****
ok: [web-002.local]
ok: [web-001.local]
```

TASK [Build webservers] ****

```
TASK [firewall : Firewall - Allow SSH connections] ****
ok: [web-002.local]
ok: [web-001.local]

TASK [firewall : Firewall - Deny everything else] ****
ok: [web-001.local]
ok: [web-002.local]

TASK [webserver : Ensure nginx is installed] ****
ok: [web-002.local]
ok: [web-001.local]

TASK [webserver : Configure nginx] ****
ok: [web-002.local]
ok: [web-001.local]

TASK [webserver : Push website content to the web root] ****
ok: [web-001.local]
ok: [web-002.local]

TASK [webserver : Firewall - Allow website connections] ****
ok: [web-001.local]
ok: [web-002.local]
```

Great. Our dependency was included. This time, the firewall role tasks appear under the main heading of "*TASK [Build webservers]*" as they are now a dependency of that role. It's important to note that the same dependency can be added to multiple roles, and Ansible will ensure that the dependency runs exactly once before those roles – if the dependency (in this case, firewall) has already run previously, Ansible by default will not run it a second time, no matter how many other roles might depend on it.

If you did require the dependency to run multiple times, once per invocation, then you could achieve that by setting the value `allow_duplicates: true` inside the meta file of the dependent role, in this case firewall, informing ansible that this role is able to be run multiple times. For our use case, this is not necessary.

Includes: Dynamic vs. Static

Throughout this chapter, we have used the `include_role` task to call our roles from the playbook. Ansible provides two ways of calling roles within the playbook, each with its own upsides and downsides. These two methods are

1. include_role – Used in our existing playbooks

2. import_role – Not used yet, for reasons we will explain

Ansible refer to `include_role` as a *dynamic* include. By contrast, `import_role` is referred to as a *static* import. The differentiation is important, as it affects how you use the role. A static import is resolved at the start of playbook execution before any tasks are run – all of the tasks, handlers, variables, etc. from the role in question are essentially copied into the playbook in one hit, as though they were written sequentially inside your main playbook. The task list, variables, and handler lists are generated and merged before *any* tasks are executed.

Because the role is imported in this way, objects such as handlers that are defined inside the role are available globally to any task in your ansible playbook, including other roles – meaning you can notify a handler inside an imported role from another role at any time.

By contrast, a dynamic include is not resolved by Ansible until it reaches the point of the `include_role` task in the playbook run. That means that at the start of playbook execution, variables and handlers from inside the role are **not** available to anything else, as they have not yet been seen by Ansible.

You can easily observe this by asking Ansible to provide a task list for the webservers.yml playbook, which uses include_role:

```
$ ansible-playbook webservers.yml --list-tasks

playbook: webservers.yml

  play #1 (webservers): webservers        TAGS: []
    tasks:
      Build webservers  TAGS: []
      Setup firewall    TAGS: []
```

Ansible only lists two tasks, the two include_role tasks that are defined in our playbook. It cannot list any of the tasks from inside those roles since it has not yet parsed them. They are not available for use until the playbook execution reaches them.

Contrast this output to that shown using import_role instead:

```
< playbook modified to use import_role >

playbook: webservers.yml

  play #1 (webservers): webservers        TAGS: []
    tasks:
      webserver : Ensure nginx is installed     TAGS: []
      webserver : Configure nginx        TAGS: []
      webserver : Push website content to the web root  TAGS: []
      webserver : Firewall - Allow website connections  TAGS: []
      firewall : Firewall - Allow SSH connections     TAGS: []
      firewall : Firewall - Deny everything else      TAGS: []
```

In contrast with include_role, since Ansible is now importing the role into its global namespace before executing anything, you can see it is aware of all the tasks inside that role.

This has some practical significance. Because they are imported exactly once at the beginning of the play, you cannot loop over an import – whereas you can loop over an include. That may or may not be significant to your playbook.

Additionally, when Ansible *imports* a role into your playbook, it must also resolve all conditionals and variables used within that role before the playbook executes. This introduces limitations in situations where you might dynamically generate some configuration, by adding a new fact learned from running a task within the playbook, for example. If Ansible hits any undefined variables during a static import, it will throw an error – meaning you need to prepare default values for all those variables used within the role even if they are to be dynamically generated later. This used to be the way things worked by default, and it was messy. You create a lot of unnecessary overhead and end up with complicated code paths.

We therefore recommend always using `include_role`, unless you have a very good reason not to. We have a lot of experience using both and generally find `include_role` to be much more flexible while not introducing too many downsides. The main cost to doing so is not being able to effectively list and use features that rely on tags or task names inside the role such as *--start-at-task*. It is useful to know that both exist and what the differences are – when using them, please try to keep in mind how the subsequent tasks are included into your play, as that will help explain their behavior while you debug your playbooks.

Old-Style Roles

While we are not using them, it is worth mentioning the old style of defining roles since you are highly likely to see this in production codebases for some years to come. `include_role` and `import_role` are relatively new (Ansible 2.3 and 2.4); before that, the accepted way to use a role from a playbook was with a different top-level keyword like `tasks:` but named `roles:` – the behavior of this was equivalent to `import_role` and not at all like `include_role`.

An example of how this would look given our current `webservers.yml` playbook:

```
---
- hosts: webservers
  become: true
  roles:
    - webserver
    - firewall
```

Be aware if using this that you are inherently using `import_role`, which imports all the elements of the role into the global playbook along with all the complications that may bring, as described earlier.

Summary

In this chapter, we brought some law and order to the chaos of our Ansible playbooks. We introduced packing cubes for your suitcase (seriously, go buy some now – we can't get enough of them!) and applied that same logic to our Ansible playbooks using roles.

Roles are perhaps one of our favorite features of Ansible. Deceptively simple, and infinitely powerful, they are the foundation of reusable code within Ansible enabling us to be lazy. The less code we need to write, the simpler the logic we can implement, the better our (and everyone else's) life will be. We walked through splitting up our existing Ansible playbook into roles, something which was more involved than you might have first imagined. We split the playbook into two roles, one for the webserver setup and one for the firewall configuration.

Toward the end of the chapter, we explored the different ways of using roles, imports and includes. We explained the practical differences and how Ansible behaves when hitting these two very different types of task. Generally, we prefer *include_role*; it is relatively easy to understand and enables some more advanced logic such as looping over the role. It does however come with some downsides, so make your choice carefully depending on your specific use case. Both are valid Ansible, and you will see many styles in the real world.

CHAPTER 10

Building a Load Balancer: Controlling Flow

With the playbooks we have built so far, we have had little need to make any key decisions or control the flow in any special way, since we are only building a single type of host – a webserver. We have seen that we can run that same playbook against multiple hosts and thus create multiple web servers. This is where Ansible really shines. At any time, we can spin up new web servers, scaling out to huge numbers of them with very little effort. We can migrate our infrastructure to a new provider at any time with a single playbook run, build staging environments to test new features, and so on.

But things can be improved. Currently, we rely on the structure of the playbook to define the ordering of tasks. That works well in a small playbook, but as they grow larger, the web of dependencies between various tasks and roles can become difficult to manage, and this often results in mistakes being made. Ansible, however, has solutions to all our problems; and for this specifically, we can control the flow through various mechanisms such as splitting our playbooks into multiple "plays," using tags which we can target (think: unique labels for sets of tasks) and conditionals to only execute specific tasks when certain conditions are met (just like an *if* statement in most programming languages).

© Shaun R Smith and Peter Membrey 2022
S. R. Smith and P. Membrey, *Beginning Ansible Concepts and Application*,
https://doi.org/10.1007/978-1-4842-8173-4_10

Other times, we may need to run a specific task only once; think generating API passwords on the local machine that can then be used across multiple target hosts – Ansible can do that too. We may wish to repeat a task several times, such as installing ten software packages using apt – it would be inefficient to define the task ten times, and we certainly don't need to.

We have touched on some of these concepts already in previous chapters; however, this chapter will explain them all in more detail. We will modify our existing playbook to show the power of tags while introducing a new system into the mix – a load balancer, enabling us to utilize both web servers while having only a single endpoint for our customers to visit. We will make use of conditionals in a variety of different forms and loop over lists to correctly configure the load balancer while allowing for infinite scale-out of our web servers. This is where we start to pull everything together and really get a working solution going.

Introducing the Load Balancer

Previously, we have built two web servers known as web-001 and web-002, and we have accessed each of them individually from a web browser to confirm that they are accepting connections as expected. In a production system, we may have many web servers, as we scale out to meet demand, and as a result we often place a load balancer in front of them to distribute incoming connections across the pool. This reduces overall load on any one server, removes a single point of failure where the web server might fail (although in our example case, we introduce a new single point of failure in the load balancer itself), and ensures that we can scale out our web servers as dictated by capacity requirements.

Note   We are deliberately keeping the setup simple to maximize your exposure to Ansible itself. The example setup here is often not the best approach to running a high-scale website but can serve as a reasonable do-it-yourself starting point.

The specific load balancer we shall use is called HAProxy (haproxy.org) which is a free open source application that is a fast and efficient load balancer. It is widely available via almost all Linux distribution's package manager, and getting started with HAProxy is relatively painless; so the choice of software won't get in our way.

We will not dive too deep into HAProxy configuration concepts, as it is beyond the scope of this book, but, essentially, there are frontends (the connections coming in from visitors) and backends (a group of application servers that execute our code and return content).

In the following diagram, we show what our target setup looks like, including the frontend (user ➤ load balancer) and backends (load balancer ➤ web servers):

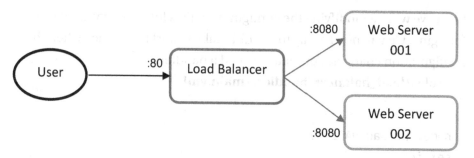

Figure 10-1. *Load Balancer Target Setup*

We will achieve this as repeatable infrastructure using Ansible playbooks and iteratively add features throughout the chapter.

Installing the Load Balancer

Building on what we have learned so far, and using the Ansible code from previous chapters, let's create a new role for the load balancer. We will name this role load_balancer:

```
> mkdir -p roles/load_balancer/{tasks,templates,handlers,meta}/
```

Note Role names should only contain the lowercase characters a–z, 0–9, and _ (underscore). The name of the role is derived from the directory name, and so we must ensure our directories meet this convention.

We will start with a simple role, which will install HAProxy, and set up basic configuration file management. Right now, it will not forward traffic to the web servers; we will add that later.

Create a New Handler for HAProxy

Since we will be modifying the configuration files for HAProxy, as we did for nginx, we will need a way to conditionally restart the service when the configuration changes. For that, we need a handler:

roles/load_balancer/handlers/main.yml

```
---
- name: Reload HAProxy
  service:
    name: haproxy
    state: reloaded
```

Add a Simple Frontend Configuration

A frontend is essential, as it tells HAProxy to listen for incoming connections on a specific port and service those requests. This configuration is extremely basic to bring up a frontend and enable HAProxy's built-in statistics endpoint so that we can confirm our installation works as expected:

roles/load_balancer/templates/frontend.cfg.j2

```
frontend awesome_ansible
    bind *:{{ http_port }}
    stats uri /haproxy?stats
```

Add the Firewall Dependency

Just as with the webservers, the load balancer depends on the core firewall to be configured for the server to operate correctly. Let's go ahead and add that dependency to the role now. For ease, we can simply copy the dependency file from the webserver's role, as it will be identical:

```
> cp roles/{webserver,load_balancer}/meta/main.yml
```

Note   The curly braces used here are a special bash convention known as brace expansion. The values inside the braces are separated by a comma and will be expanded out into two separate text strings or parameters, resulting in the command:

```
cp roles/webserver/.. roles/load_balancer/..
```

Bringing It Together

We will introduce a new module called *assemble* in the following role. We use this because HAProxy does not support multiple configuration file snippets natively, and so to ensure our configuration is dynamic and easy to manage, we use the *assemble* module to concatenate (merge together) multiple configuration files into the single *haproxy.cfg* file required.

We will also introduce some more advanced concepts, such as not overriding a file when it already exists by using the force: no option on the *copy* module and validating the resulting configuration file after assembling it by passing a validation command to the *assemble* module. Let's put it all into action and see what it looks like:

roles/load_balancer/tasks/main.yml

```
---
- name: Install HAProxy
  apt:
    name: haproxy
    state: present
    cache_valid_time: 60

- name: Create configuration directory
  file:
    path: /etc/haproxy/fragments
    state: directory

- name: Copy original configuration file
  copy:
    src: /etc/haproxy/haproxy.cfg
    dest: /etc/haproxy/fragments/00_defaults.cfg
    remote_src: yes
    force: no
```

```
- name: Setup frontends
  template:
    src: frontends.cfg.j2
    dest: /etc/haproxy/fragments/40_frontends.cfg

- name: Build configuration from fragments
  assemble:
    src: /etc/haproxy/fragments/
    dest: /etc/haproxy/haproxy.cfg
    validate: "haproxy -f %s -c"
  notify: Reload HAProxy

- name: Firewall - Allow website connections
  ufw:
    rule: allow
    port: "{{ http_port }}"
```

load_balancers.yml

```
---
- hosts: load_balancers
  become: true
  tasks:
    - name: Build load balancers
      include_role:
        name: load_balancer
```

You may wonder why we are using plural *load_balancers* for the host group and singular *load_balancer* for the role name. That is because the role is used to configure a single load balancer, but it may be applied to multiple hosts contained in the host group *load_balancers*.

Build the Load Balancer

Now run the load_balancers.yml playbook, and if all the above went well, you should immediately have a working HAProxy installation. Pretty nice for such little effort!

You may need to bring the load balancer host up via vagrant if you have not already done so. Go ahead and do that now on your local machine:

```
> vagrant up lb-001
```

Then from the ansible controller (using vagrant ssh controller):

```
> ansible-playbook load_balancers.yml

PLAY [load_balancers] ****

TASK [Gathering Facts] ****
ok: [lb-001.local]

TASK [Setup Firewall] ****

TASK [firewall : Firewall - Allow SSH connections] ****
changed: [lb-001.local]

TASK [firewall : Firewall - Deny everything else] ****
changed: [lb-001.local]

TASK [Build load balancers] ****

TASK [load_balancer : Install HAProxy] ****
changed: [lb-001.local]

TASK [load_balancer : Create configuration directory] ****
changed: [lb-001.local]

TASK [load_balancer : Copy original configuration file] ****
changed: [lb-001.local]
```

```
TASK [load_balancer : Setup frontends] ****
changed: [lb-001.local]

TASK [load_balancer : Build configuration from fragments] ****
changed: [lb-001.local]

TASK [load_balancer : Firewall - Allow website
connections] ****
changed: [lb-001.local]

RUNNING HANDLER [load_balancer : Reload HAProxy] ****
changed: [lb-001.local]
```

Verify That It Worked

Assuming all went to plan, and the playbook completed as expected, you should now have a running HAProxy service with stats enabled. You can access the stats from HAProxy via the frontend, meaning you can browse to it using your web browser by pointing it at the following URL:

```
http://lb-001.local/haproxy?stats
```

or

```
http://192.168.98.121/haproxy?stats
```

You should be presented with a page showing stats for the frontend that we created earlier, named *awesome_ansible*.

HAProxy version 2.0.13-2ubuntu0.1, released 2020/09/08

Statistics Report for pid 18904

> General process information

	active UP		backup UP
pid = 18904 (process #1, nbproc = 1, nbthread = 1)	active UP, going down		backup UP, going down
uptime = 0d 0h01m48s	active DOWN, going up		backup DOWN, going up
system limits: memmax = unlimited; ulimit-n = 1023	active or backup DOWN		not checked
maxsock = 1023; maxconn = 493; maxpipes = 0			
current conns = 3; current pipes = 0/0; conn rate = 2/sec; bit rate = 0.000 kbps	active or backup DOWN for maintenance (MAINT)		
Running tasks: 2/13; idle = 100 %	active or backup SOFT STOPPED for maintenance		

Note: "NOLB"/"DRAIN" = UP with load-balancing disabled.

awesome_ansible

	Queue			Session rate			Sessions						Bytes		Denied		Errors		
	Cur	Max	Limit	Cur	Max	Limit	Cur	Max	Limit	Total	LbTot	Last	In	Out	Req	Resp	Req	Conn	Resp
Frontend				2	2	-	3	3	493	3			238	81	0	0	0		

Figure 10-2. HAProxy stats output

Setting Up Backends: Looping in Config Templates

To make our load balancer useful, it needs to talk to the backend web servers to be able to serve content. In HAProxy parlance, a group of servers to which connections are handed off is known as a *backend*.

We have a single backend pool, which is comprised of two webservers. HAProxy needs to understand how to reach both of those webservers, and so Ansible will need to push that configuration to the load balancer; however, what is really important here is that the configuration is *dynamic*. When we add more webservers to our setup later, we don't want to have to manually modify a configuration file somewhere in our load_balancer role; we want it to automatically pick up the change and reconfigure the load balancer for us.

This is where loops come in. There are broadly two ways of looping in Ansible:

1. Using loop/with_items parameters on a task (used later)

2. Within a template, which we will use now

Create Backends

Let's create a new configuration template for backends and take a quick look at how we can define a loop to set up our backend webservers dynamically:

roles/load_balancer/templates/backends.cfg.j2

```
backend web_servers
    balance roundrobin
    {% for host in groups.webservers %}
    server {{ host }} {{ host }}:{{ hostvars[host].http_port }}
    {% endfor %}
```

Note   We are using a special variable hostvars to access variables, or facts, that are assigned directly to the specific host we are parsing. In this way, we know the unique IP and port for each webserver.

Add this task to the role directly below the *Setup frontends* task:

```
- name: Setup frontends
  template:
    src: frontends.cfg.j2
    dest: /etc/haproxy/fragments/40_frontends.cfg

- name: Setup backends
  template:
    src: backends.cfg.j2
    dest: "/etc/haproxy/fragments/90_backends.cfg"
```

Wire the Frontend to the Backend

To wire up the frontend to the backend, we need to modify the frontends template at roles/load_balancer/templates/frontends.cfg.j2 as follows:

```
frontend awesome_ansible
    bind *:{{ http_port }}
    stats enable
    default_backend web_servers
```

Execute the Playbook

```
> ansible-playbook load_balancers.yml
```

The result of running this playbook will be a file on the server named /etc/haproxy/fragments/backends.cfg with the content:

```
> ssh lb-001.local cat /etc/haproxy/fragments/backends.cfg

backend web_servers
    balance roundrobin
        server web-001.local web-001.local:8080
        server web-002.local web-002.local:8080
```

Visit the frontend via a web browser, and you should be served content from the webserver backend:

```
http://lb-001.local/
```

or

```
http://192.168.98.121/
```

You should see your website content from one of the web servers. As we configured the backend to load balance using round-robin, refreshing the page should result in the content being delivered from the alternate webservers web-001 and web-002 consecutively. You can tell that thanks to the hostname we added to index.html for each web server earlier.

Congratulations – you have a working load balancer!

Bringing It Together

We explained at the beginning of the book that a playbook can contain multiple plays, a set of tasks that are grouped by a set of target hosts. However, what we have built are two distinct playbooks for each type of hosts: *webservers* and *load_balancers*.

If we look closely at both the webservers.yml and load_balancers.yml playbooks, you may notice some similarities:

1. We run our firewall role twice, in each playbook, one as a dependency and one as an explicit include_ role. We did not adhere to the DRY (don't repeat yourself) principle.

2. Both playbooks look remarkably similar.

We also introduced some interdependence between these playbooks. The load balancers are configured with dynamic backend configuration, which will change depending on how many webservers exist. With the current playbook format, one would be required to execute both webservers.yml *and* load_balancers.yml anytime a change is made to the webserver's configuration (such as adding a new webserver or changing a port number).

We therefore want to combine them into a single playbook that we run once. But each role targets a different set of host groups, so how can we ensure we only provision webservers using the web server roles, while the load balancer uses the load_balancer role? Enter multiple plays.

Multiple plays allow us to control the flow of our playbooks explicitly by using all the familiar building blocks, such as include_role tasks, which are grouped into a play. Remember a play links the tasks and roles with a set of target hosts.

For the current playbook, we will define two plays:

1. Target webservers host group with the webserver role

2. Target load_balancers host group with the load_balancer role

Build a single Provision Playbook

To achieve this, we can combine all our existing playbooks into one while migrating the duplicated firewall include_role to a new play:

provision.yml

```
---
- hosts: webservers
  become: true
  tasks:
    - name: Build webservers
      include_role:
        name: webserver

- hosts: load_balancers
  become: true
```

```
tasks:
  - name: Build load balancers
    include_role:
      name: load_balancer
```

Execute the Provision Playbook

When executing this playbook, Ansible will work through each of the plays we have specified sequentially, meaning the firewall will be provisioned across all hosts before moving on to the next play which sets up the web servers before finally configuring the load balancer.

This ordering makes sense when considering the load balancer backs onto the web servers, so we need those to be up and available before the load balancer is useful. All the hosts depend on the basic firewall setup, so we place that play first in the playbook, and there is no need to remember which sequence is correct when you return to these playbooks in the future.

Run the new playbook (we will not include the output since it should be familiar by now):

```
> ansible-playbook provision.yml
```

Playing Tag

Structured playbooks are great; it is extremely clear what will be run and in which order just from reading the high-level playbook. The roles are defined in such a way that they describe an outcome rather than an action and the playbook tells a story. However, beneath this smooth finery lies a murky little detail.

Think of the case where we add a new default firewall rule to allow access to a new management tool or perhaps change the SSH port. We would need to perform a full playbook run against every host, reconfiguring the web servers, possibly restarting services (depending on how our playbooks are designed), and broadly wasting a lot of time. This is especially true as we scale out and hit remote servers around the world. The firewall tasks are scattered throughout various roles, but wouldn't it be better if we could run *only* those tasks that were necessary to update the firewall rules, and leave everything else well alone?

One could achieve this by having all firewall rules inside a single firewall role. But that does not feel right – we would lose the flexibility of each service we operate having its own role and reduce their reusability. For example, we may want to configure the webserver to listen on port 443 using TLS and would like this firewall rule to live within the webserver role such that updating these interrelated configurations is obvious, easy to manage, and reusable. Conversely, we would need the SSH port defined in a single central location, since it is consistent across all hosts and is unrelated to the webserver or load balancer component. Enter *tags*.

A tag is simply a label assigned to a task, only we can target specific tags when running our playbooks with the result that only tasks that have been assigned that tag are executed. All other tasks are skipped. By adding a `tag: firewall` to all tasks related to firewall configuration across all of our roles, we can realize the ability to change firewall settings without touching anything else.

Add a Firewall Tag

We need to find and modify all our firewall rules. That includes those that appear in the `webserver`, `load_balancer`, and `firewall` roles. You'll need to add the tag `firewall` to each task in the following way:

```
- name: Firewall - Allow website connections
  ufw:
    rule: allow
    port: "{{ http_port }}"
  tags:
    - firewall
```

In YAML, `tags` defined in this way are a list of values whereby each element (denoted by a hyphen) will be applied to the task. You can also assign a single tag as a string, but the authors prefer to design for change later – thus, creating a list up front makes more sense.

Because we are using `include_role` (dynamic includes) which are parsed at runtime and not precomputed, and those `include_role` definitions are just tasks in Ansible, if we do not assign them a tag then they will not match and thus not executed at all when targeting a tag such as *firewall*. Obviously, assigning the firewall tag to the *webserver* and *load_balancer* `include_role` definitions does not make much sense, since they are not specifically firewall roles; but that is the expected way to pass through tags. We don't however want to manage a full inventory of tags both inside the role and at the playbook level. So we need to tell Ansible to *always* include *all* roles such that we always have access to tags within those roles. This is a complexity that did not used to exist and can be quite confusing to wrap your head around – thankfully, the solution is simple, but not elegant.

We achieve this by adding a special tag called *always* to each `include_role`. There is also an opposing special tag *never*, which results in the task never being run during an Ansible play.

Add the always tag to all `include_role` in the `provision.yml` playbook.

Example:

```
- hosts: webservers
  become: true
  tasks:
    - name: Build webservers
      include_role:
        name: webserver
      tags:
        - always

- hosts: load_balancers
  become: true
  tasks:
    - name: Build load balancers
      include_role:
        name: load_balancer
      tags:
        - always
```

We are walking through this only to give the full breadth of how tags and include_role interact. There are myriad ways to configure things and structure your playbooks, and we really do recommend reading much more around import_role, include_role, and their impact on tags, among other things, to truly understand where and when to use each effectively.

Executing Only Firewall Tasks

To execute the playbook run, and *include* only those tasks with the new tag *firewall*, simply provide the additional tags parameter:

```
ansible-playbook provision.yml --tags firewall
```

Skipping Firewall Tasks

Conversely, to skip all tasks that have the tag firewall, you can simply pass the skip-tags parameter to ansible-playbook:

```
ansible-playbook provision.yml --skip-tags firewall
```

Firewall Rules Using Loops

We haven't yet set up HTTPS to avoid the complexity of certificate generation and management, but suppose for a moment we had. The firewall rule task currently defines only a single rule for the value of http_port which defaults to port 80 in group_vars/all and is overridden to 8080 for the webservers in group_vars/webservers.

If we were to then set up HTTPS alongside HTTP, which operates on port 443, we would need to define an additional firewall rule. However, we do not need to define an additional task as Ansible allows looping over a single task with different input values using a keyword called loop.

Note   You may previously have come across various incantations of with_* such as with_items, with_dict, etc. While they are still valid, Ansible v2.5 introduced the loop keyword which is now recommended for most use cases.

Add an https_port

First, let's add a default https_port variable to group_vars/all:

```
---
http_port: 80
https_port: 443
```

Now we can modify the load balancer's firewall task to loop over the values for http_port and https_port by specifying them as a YAML list. Modify roles/load_balancer/tasks/main.yml as follows:

```
- name: Firewall - Allow website connections
  ufw:
    rule: allow
    port: "{{ item }}"
  loop:
    - "{{ http_port }}"
    - "{{ https_port }}"
  tags:
    - firewall
```

Execute Firewall Tasks

Using the firewall tag created earlier, execute the playbook limiting tasks to those with the firewall tag:

```
> ansible-playbook provision.yml --tags firewall
```

This time, the task to configure the firewall rules for the load balancer will look quite different to previous playbook runs:

```
TASK [load_balancer : Firewall - Allow website
connections] ****
ok: [lb-001.local] => (item=80)
changed: [lb-001.local] => (item=443)
```

We can see in the output that the task was executed twice, once with the value of item set to 80 (http_port) and again with the value of item set to 443 (https_port). As such, **both** firewall rules will now exist on the target host.

Summary

Congratulations. All these small steps have resulted in something monumental – you now have two web servers, which can scale out at the touch of a button fronted by a round-robin load balancer which is handling all incoming connections and is dynamically configured to map onto as many backend web servers as you provide. The firewall on each host is configured exactly as needed and can be targeted or excluded as needed on each playbook run.

We used some more advanced concepts to manage the HAProxy configuration file with fragments and the assemble module. We looped over multiple items both inside a configuration template (looping over members of a group and using host variables) and within a task using the loop keyword to configure multiple firewall ports on the load balancer. Hopefully, you also picked up some basic HAProxy along the way.

Now that we have a fully functioning web stack, the next chapter will focus on making it useful. We will deploy a WordPress website to our webservers and dive into some basic security by adding TLS to our load balancer frontend, which stretches our ansible skills even further by needing to generate certificates. We will then *destroy* our entire stack and rebuild it from scratch using the Ansible playbooks we have created throughout the book so far to show how easy such a seemingly dangerous and insurmountable feat becomes.

CHAPTER 11

Running a Blog

We now have two fully functioning web servers, with a load balancer distributing incoming connections between each of them. The next step is making this useful with a content management system. In this chapter, we will work through installing and configuring our first blog using WordPress in a setup that utilizes everything we have built so far. If you are just jumping in at this point and do not have the current Ansible playbooks available, you can find all the code for the previous chapter in our source code repository documented at the start of this book.

To set up a working WordPress website, we will need

1. A database to store credentials and blog posts

2. Changes to the load balancer to benefit from health checks, which ensure we only send requests to healthy webservers, and persistent sessions, to ensure repeat connections from the same user always go to the same web server

3. WordPress itself, installed on both web servers

With that in mind, let's get to work.

© Shaun R Smith and Peter Membrey 2022
S. R. Smith and P. Membrey, *Beginning Ansible Concepts and Application*,
https://doi.org/10.1007/978-1-4842-8173-4_11

A Note About Credentials

In the interests of time and complexity, we will initially be storing credentials in plaintext throughout this chapter. This is something we would **never** do in any production system (or dev/staging for that matter) as our secrets should never touch a disk unencrypted lest they fall into the wrong hands. We will be diving into how to secure your credentials in the next chapter.

PHP on the Webservers

First, we need to ensure PHP is available on our webservers, since WordPress is a PHP application. To do so, we will modify our existing webservers role to additionally install and set up a package named php-fpm, a module which enables the web server nginx to execute PHP code directly.

To install a second package, we could use a loop with the apt install task; however, certain modules have optimizations to improve performance when operating over multiple elements. apt is one such module. Rather than looping over the Ansible task (and thus running apt multiple times on the target host), we can instead pass a list of package names directly to the apt module, resulting in a single apt command on the host to install all listed packages. This results in a significant speedup.

To do so, edit `roles/webserver/tasks/main.yml`:

```
- name: Ensure nginx and php are installed
  apt:
    name:
      - nginx
      - php-fpm
      - php-mysql
    state: present
```

We also need to instruct nginx to use the new php-fpm module, which is a simple change to our configuration template:

roles/webservers/templates/nginx-default.j2

```
# force a config reload
server {
        listen {{ http_port }} default_server;

        root /var/www/html;

        # Use the default catch-all server name
        server_name _;
        {% if status_url is defined -%}
        location /{{ status_url }} {
            stub_status on;
        }
        {%- endif %}

        index index.php index.html index.htm;

        location ~ \.php$ {
            include snippets/fastcgi-php.conf;
            fastcgi_pass unix:/var/run/php/php-fpm.sock;
        }
}
```

Set Up a Database Server
Exercise: Build a Database Role

Try to set up a database server yourself. Here is what you will need:

1. A new inventory group called databases with the
    server db-001.local such that Ansible can talk to it.
    Take inspiration from the webservers inventory file.

2. A role called database, which for now can simply
    install the MySQL package mysql-server and the
    python module to enable Ansible to manage it:
    python3-pymysql.

3. A firewall rule allowing port 3306 on the
    database server.

4. A handler named "Restart MySQL" which we can
    trigger when making configuration changes. This
    should restart, not reload, MySQL. We will cover
    the actual configuration later. [Hint: The service is
    named mysql.]

5. A new play in provision.yml targeting the
    databases host group with the new database role.

6. Start the database server using vagrant up db-001.

7. Provision it with Ansible.

If you struggle with any of the preceding list, refer to the related files in
Chapter 11 of the source code repository shared at the start of the book.

Add Database Configuration

Before we create a database, or attempt to install WordPress using the
database credentials, we need to have access to the details of the database
from multiple Ansible roles, namely, database and wordpress. That is
because we need to configure the relevant user account on the database
server and then point wordpress at the database server, authenticating
using those same credentials.

To achieve this, we will add the credentials to the inventory/group_vars/all file, meaning they are available to all hosts within our Ansible inventory:

```
---
http_port: 80
https_port: 443

database:
    host: db-001.local
    name: wordpress
    username: wordpress_rw
    password: SomeSuperStrongPassword
root_password: EvenStrongerPassword
```

We are using a YAML dictionary to group the related elements of configuration. This is a great way to arrange configuration items, as we can then refer to them by their dictionary name.key such as database.username.

Extend the New Database Role

Hopefully, you managed to get a basic database role created, which installs the required MySQL packages onto the database server db-001.local along with a simple handler to restart it when needed. We do not yet have any tasks that notify the handler, as we have not made any configuration changes yet.

Now we will extend the new role to configure MySQL and create various user credentials for use by our future WordPress installation, using Ansible modules designed just for this purpose.

You will need to add these new tasks to your database role, which should live at roles/database/tasks/main.yml:

```yaml
---
- name: Install MySQL
  apt:
    name:
      - mysql-server
      - python3-pymysql
    state: present

- name: Set the root password
  mysql_user:
    name: root
    password: "{{ database.root_password }}"
    state: present
    login_user: root
    login_password: "{{database.root_password }}"
    login_unix_socket: /var/run/mysqld/mysqld.sock
  no_log: True

- name: Create the wordpress database
  mysql_db:
    name: "{{ database.name }}"
    state: present
    login_user: root
    login_password: "{{database.root_password }}"

- name: Create the wordpress user
  mysql_user:
    name: "{{ database.username }}"
    password: "{{database.password }}"
    priv: "{{ database.name }}.*:ALL"
    host: "%"
```

```
   state: present
   login_user: root
   login_password: "{{database.root_password }}"
  no_log: True

- name: Ensure MySQL listens on the network
  lineinfile:
    path: /etc/mysql/mysql.conf.d/mysqld.cnf
    regexp: '^bind-address'
    line: 'bind-address = 0.0.0.0'
  notify:
    - Restart MySQL

- name: Firewall - Allow database connections
  ufw:
    rule: allow
    port: "3306"
  tags:
    - firewall
```

The mysql_* Modules

Ansible provides several modules for managing MySQL servers, such that you can directly create databases and users, set variables, and perform queries against MySQL servers in an Ansible-friendly manner. Here, we are using two such modules:

1. mysql_user for creating, deleting, and editing database users

2. mysql_db for creating, deleting, and editing databases

Many of the parameters are completed using variables, as we define the database name, hostname, username, password, and root_password (for management) in a YAML dictionary which is shared across multiple roles via group_vars. You'll notice there are some unique parameters for these modules, which are specific to MySQL, namely:

1. login_user / login_password – The username and password that are used to connect to MySQL to perform the administrative actions. This user must be privileged and able to create/modify databases and/or users.

2. login_unix_socket – This is used only on the first mysql_user task, where we set the root user's password. At this point, the root user does not have a password set, and so we are not able to log in via the network to perform administrative actions; therefore, we use a special file known as a UNIX socket to connect to the MySQL service.

3. priv / host – These are specific MySQL nomenclature, meaning privileges (or what the user has access to) and which hosts the user can log in *from*. If you do not specify this, it defaults to localhost and will *not* allow remote connections, such as those from the webservers.

Load Balancer Backend Persistence

As we are about to start working with a dynamic application, which uses cookies and has authentication, we need to ensure that a single user session will not be load balanced across multiple different servers. The reason for this is that our session state is stored on the webserver that we first hit. If a subsequent request then hits the other webserver, it would have the effect of creating a new session, and thus logging us out, or losing track of our session state.

Thankfully, this is a common problem, and so HAProxy has support for a feature known as session persistence out of the box. We will also add health checks – a simple HTTP request that will be made by the load balancer to the backend webserver to ensure it is still available and serving requests. The result of this is that when a webserver fails, or shuts down for maintenance, the load balancer will simply mark it as failed and not serve any new requests from that webserver until it returns. We can enable both features by modifying the template:

roles/load_balancer/templates/backends.cfg.j2

```
backend web_servers
    balance roundrobin
    cookie SERVERID insert indirect nocache
    {% for host in groups.webservers %}
    server {{ host }} {{ host }}:{{ hostvars[host].http_port }}
check cookie {{ host }}
    {% endfor %}
```

Let's take a look at these additions.

```
cookie SERVERID insert indirect nocache
```

This line instructs HAProxy to set a new cookie on initial request identifying the server that was selected using round-robin, such that the cookie will be available to subsequent requests.

```
check cookie {{ host }}
```

The check keyword instructs HAProxy to perform health checks against the backend server to ensure it is still available and remove it from the pool if it is not. The following cookie <name> informs HAProxy that the host should be matched against cookies with that SERVERID set, meaning all subsequent requests using a cookie with the relevant SERVERID will also be sent to the relevant backend server.

Install WordPress

WordPress is a free and open source content management system which was originally designed as a blog management system but over the years has been extended to cater to many different use cases. Today, it powers a significant number of diverse websites around the world; WordPress is used in some form on 41% of the top ten million websites globally[1] as of April 2021.

It is written in PHP and uses a MySQL database to store its authentication and managed content; so we now have everything we need to successfully install WordPress onto our web servers.

Create the WordPress Role

The WordPress role will be responsible for downloading, installing, and configuring WordPress inside the webserver's web root directory. To achieve this, we will introduce a new Ansible module named unarchive. This module is designed for extracting archive files such as zip or gzip into a given destination directory while setting relevant owners, groups, and permissions on the resulting files and directories.

Create the new role as roles/wordpress/tasks/main.yml:

```
---
- name: Download and unarchive Wordpress
  unarchive:
    src: https://wordpress.org/latest.tar.gz
```

---

[1] https://w3techs.com/technologies/overview/content_management

```
    remote_src: True
    owner: root
    group: www-data
    dest: "/var/www/html/"
    creates: "/var/www/html/wordpress"
- name: Configure Wordpress
  template:
    src: "wp-config.php.j2"
    dest: "/var/www/html/wordpress/wp-config.php"
    owner: root
    group: www-data
mode: 'u=rw,g=r,o='
```

You will see a couple of interesting parameters used on these modules to manage permissions. These all have a specific purpose:

1. remote_src – This instructs the unarchive module to look for the src archive on the remote server and not on the local ansible controller. The default would be to find the archive locally, push it to the target host, and then unarchive it.

2. creates – Passing this option with a filename to the module instructs Ansible to only execute the task if that file does **not** exist. When the file does exist, Ansible will skip this task. It is only appropriate for modules that otherwise have no way to know if they should execute, such as unarchive, shell, command, etc.

3. owner / group / mode – These fields instruct Ansible to create files using the relevant file attributes such as the user and group that own the file and the access permissions.

Create a wp-config.php.j2 Template

In the source code repository that contains the Vagrantfile, we have included the wp-config.php.j2 template file needed for this step. You can copy it from there to the roles/wordpress/templates/ directory. We did this because it is cumbersome to type it all out – WordPress expects several randomly generated secret keys along with some boilerplate, and there is no good way around this.

For reference, the file content is as follows:

```php
<?php

// ** MySQL settings ** //
define('DB_NAME', '{{ database.name }}');
define('DB_USER', '{{ database.username }}');
define('DB_PASSWORD', '{{ database.password }}');
define('DB_HOST', '{{ database.host }}');

// ** Authentication Unique Keys ** //
define('AUTH_KEY', '{{ lookup('password',
    '/dev/null length=128') }}');

define('SECURE_AUTH_KEY', '{{ lookup('password',
    '/dev/null length=128') }}');

define('LOGGED_IN_KEY', '{{ lookup('password',
    '/dev/null length=128') }}');

define('NONCE_KEY', '{{ lookup('password',
    '/dev/null length=128') }}');

// ** WordPress Database Table prefix. ** //
$table_prefix = 'wp_';
```

```php
/** Absolute path to the WordPress directory. */
if ( ! defined( 'ABSPATH' ) ) {
    define( 'ABSPATH', __DIR__ . '/' );
}

/** Sets up WordPress vars and included files. */
require_once ABSPATH . 'wp-settings.php';
```

Add Role to the Webservers Play

Finally, we must add the new wordpress role to our playbook. As we need WordPress to be installed onto the webservers, it makes sense to add the wordpress role to the webservers play.

Modify the file provision.yml:

```yaml
- hosts: webservers
  become: true
  tasks:
    - name: Build webservers
      include_role:
        name: webserver
      tags:
        - always

    - name: Install Wordpress
      include_role:
        name: wordpress
      tags:
        - always
```

Complete Installation

That is all there is to it. The playbooks that we have created thus far should fully configure a database server, the load balancer, and the web servers and install and configure WordPress. The only remaining step to get started with WordPress is to browse to it via the web browser and configure your first user account.

Visit the new WordPress website via the load balancer:

```
http://lb-001.local/wordpress/
```

or

```
http://192.168.98.121/wordpress/
```

You should be presented with the screen shown in Figure 11-1, which you can complete using the details you deem suitable.

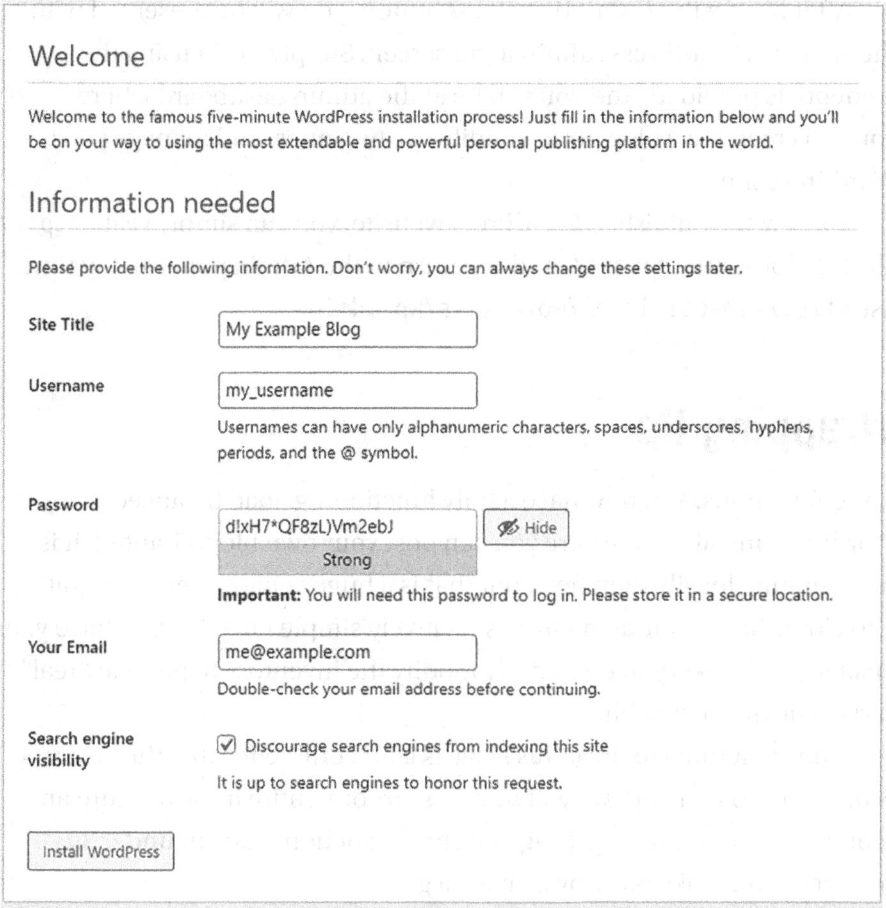

Welcome

Welcome to the famous five-minute WordPress installation process! Just fill in the information below and you'll be on your way to using the most extendable and powerful personal publishing platform in the world.

Information needed

Please provide the following information. Don't worry, you can always change these settings later.

Site Title	My Example Blog
Username	my_username
	Usernames can have only alphanumeric characters, spaces, underscores, hyphens, periods, and the @ symbol.
Password	d!xH7*QF8zL)Vm2ebJ 👁 Hide
	Strong
	Important: You will need this password to log in. Please store it in a secure location.
Your Email	me@example.com
	Double-check your email address before continuing.
Search engine visibility	☑ Discourage search engines from indexing this site
	It is up to search engines to honor this request.

Install WordPress

Figure 11-1. *The WordPress setup wizard for initial user creation*

If you get a 403 or 502, it is highly likely that you either forgot to install the php-fpm packages in the webserver role or that you did not add the relevant configuration to the `nginx-default.conf.j2` template.

After hitting the *Install WordPress* button, you will be presented with the standard WordPress Admin login screen. Simply log in using the credentials provided, and you will be at the admin dashboard where you can create new blog posts, modify existing ones, and manage your WordPress site.

To view the published WordPress website, you can simply visit `http://lb-001.local/wordpress/`, and to return to the Admin panel at any time, use `http://lb-001.local/wordpress/wp-admin/`.

Wrapping Up

Congratulations. You now have a fully functioning, load balanced WordPress installation where you can post your own blog. Granted, it is only running locally right now, but that is a huge achievement – migrating it to cloud-hosted infrastructure is relatively simple now that you have your ansible playbooks; you can simply modify the inventory to point at "real" servers or virtual machines.

One great thing to do at this stage is gain confidence that this really is the case. To that end, we will now destroy our entire infrastructure and rebuild it from scratch – getting back to production ready in under 30 minutes. Don't take our word; give it a go.

```
> vagrant destroy web-001 web-002, lb-001, db-001
> vagrant up
```

Note   vagrant up will take some time, as it needs to reprovision all of the destroyed hosts, including software installations.

Now, connect back into your ansible controller and run the playbook:

```
> vagrant ssh controller
> cd /vagrant
> ansible-playbook provision.yml
```

That's it! Once again, visit the load balancer address and re-set up WordPress, and you should be ready to roll once again.

Summary

This chapter is the culmination of all our hard work to this point. We now have an industry standard content management system running on two web servers, which can be scaled out to three or more at any time. We have a shared database server which stores all user credentials and content. We have a load balancer, which is distributing incoming connections across the multiple backend web servers in a round-robin fashion, with health checks bringing the web servers in or out of the pool accordingly and session persistence to ensure WordPress can track our session correctly and keep us logged in.

Even better than all of that, we can destroy the entire setup, run a single playbook, `provision.yml`, and be up and running again in *minutes*. We can scale at will, by adding more hosts. We can migrate our entire setup to physical or virtual machines running anywhere in the world.[2]

Next, we will delve into the more advanced topics of Ansible, such as how to secure your secrets using Vaults and expanding your Ansible power by leveraging community-provided modules via Galaxy.

---

[2] We would not recommend doing this right now, as communications between the user, load balancer, web servers, and database server are not secured.

CHAPTER 12

Locking Away Your Secrets: Vaults

In the previous chapter, we stored various credentials such as the database username and password in plaintext. That would be like storing hoards of gold bullion in your bedside table at home and hoping that anybody breaking into your home doesn't find it. Pushing those credentials to version control would be like painting a huge sign on your house announcing, "The gold is here." Let's not do that.

If you did happen to have huge amounts of gold bullion, I'm sure you'd either invest in a safe or otherwise be speaking to your bank manager about a secure Vault with the bank. The idea is you can take all your valuable possessions and place them inside a box secured by a passphrase or a key to which only you have access – safely away from prying eyes. To gain access, you need to supply the key or passphrase. The same applies to your digital secrets.

The downside to a Vault is that you need to physically access it every time you need access to what's inside. The same is true digitally, except it is much easier because the encrypted content can be stored alongside your code. There is no need for physical separation.

The power of having those credentials available to our Ansible playbooks in a central location and accessible by our playbooks and configuration templates is critical to automation – it allows our playbooks to be executed with little human interaction.

© Shaun R Smith and Peter Membrey 2022
S. R. Smith and P. Membrey, *Beginning Ansible Concepts and Application*,
https://doi.org/10.1007/978-1-4842-8173-4_12

Thankfully, Ansible provides such a feature out of the box – unsurprisingly called a Vault. An Ansible vault is a normal file on your disk which you can edit using your favorite text editor, with one key difference. When you hit save, the file is automatically locked up inside strong AES-256 encryption. The plaintext version exists in memory (RAM) only while you are editing, and the file is immediately encrypted again before being saved to disk – safe from prying eyes.

Ansible Vaults protect data *at rest*, the plaintext contents of the Vault will be decrypted during playbook execution, and any Ansible modules or plugins used will have direct access to them.

Before we start, let's examine the two types of Vaults that exist and what they are used for:

1. Inline – An encrypted string stored in an otherwise plaintext YAML configuration file. Metadata such as variable names are stored in plaintext and can be read, while secret contents are encrypted.

2. File – A file that has been encrypted as a single binary blob; none of the contents can be read without first decrypting the entire file.

You will almost certainly use both throughout your Ansible journey, as each has its own benefits and downsides. For example, a great use case for inline vaults is configuration files, such as the storing of API keys. That is because

1. Your encrypted variables can be stored alongside your unencrypted variables, reducing cognitive overhead. For example, encrypted passwords are in the same file as the unencrypted username.

2. You can search for variable names within your
    playbooks using features such as `git grep`
    and quickly see where they are defined. This is
    impossible with a fully encrypted file.

On the other hand, a fully encrypted binary file makes much more
sense where the data that you are encrypting is not a configuration file, but
a data file. This is often the case if you are storing things such as TLS keys.
Some benefits of this include

1. All vaults that can be decrypted with the key
    provided at runtime will be decrypted by Ansible
    automatically, making the data available to all your
    playbooks.

2. The encrypted vault can live next to the code that
    uses it, such as inside your role, and can be a *file*, a
    template, or any other valid Ansible file, meaning
    your playbook can simply use the file as normal
    within a task, but it is safely encrypted at rest
    on disk.

With that background out of the way, we can dive into the command
for managing vaults: `ansible-vault`.

Diving into Vaults
Creating Your First Vault

Running the `ansible-vault` command, we can see that there are several
actions available:

```
create          Create new vault encrypted file
decrypt         Decrypt vault encrypted file
edit            Edit vault encrypted file
```

```
view              View vault encrypted file
encrypt           Encrypt YAML file
encrypt_string    Encrypt a string
rekey             Re-key a vault encrypted file
```

Some of these actions have an obvious function, such as create a new vault; decrypt, edit, rekey, or view an existing vault; or encrypt an existing file, which will convert a plaintext file to a vault.

Then there is the action encrypt_string. The former are all involved in the management of a Vault file – creating, editing, and viewing the contents of the vault; the latter is an interesting action that does not have a view or decrypt counterpart. This is used for the creation of what we call *inline vault* values. We will explore these in more detail later.

For the time being, let's use the basic functions to create and view a vault file using the ansible-vault command:

```
> ansible-vault create my_vault.yml

New Vault password: test [enter]
Confirm New Vault password: test [enter]
```

Having been asked for a new password twice, you will be presented with an empty file in your configured text editor (for me, that is vim). For now, you can type anything into this file. Try a memorable phrase. I used "Ansible Vaults are so cool!". Save the file and exit your text editor.

Tip   If you're not familiar with vim, then you may want to consult a Getting Started guide at https://medium.com/swlh/getting-started-with-vim-3f11fc4f62c4.

Earlier, we claimed that, upon saving, this file would be automatically encrypted using AES-256. Let's confirm that this is the case by looking at the file we just created. To do so, we will use the cat tool, which simply prints out the file's contents:

```
> cat my_vault.yml
$ANSIBLE_VAULT;1.1;AES256
37393730343134633733646237633865563643335646438623073962643534
636631333562336465
64386664353033396532613063366634643135396430626640a386666343739
366266306635643462
```

Here, you see that the file has a *header line* – the first line in the file that defines some metadata or information on what the file is and how it can be understood. This header line tells us that this is an Ansible Vault, versioned as 1.1 and using the AES-256 encryption scheme. What follows are series digits, which are the encrypted contents of your file. The message that you typed is not clearly visible in the resulting file.

To view the plaintext contents of the vault, you will also need to use the ansible-vault command to decrypt the file. You will be prompted to enter the password for the vault file that you used when creating it:

```
> ansible-vault view my_vault.yml
Vault password: test [enter]
Ansible Vaults are so cool!
```

If you need, you can modify this file to your heart's content using the ansible-vault edit command. This will again request your original vault password before being able to decrypt the contents to edit:

```
> ansible-vault view my_vault.yml
Vault password: test [enter]
```

This will, once again, drop you into your configured text editor and upon saving will automatically encrypt the contents of the file just as create did earlier.

The key point to take away from this section is an Ansible vault can contain *any* data. There is no specific format for a vault file – it is simply an encrypted container around absolutely any data you would like to include. Often, the content will be a YAML file, but not always. This makes it incredibly versatile.

You can encrypt configuration files for web servers, database schemas, website contents, all the way to SSL private keys, a sensitive binary file that is needed on a server. Really, anything.

Vault IDs

Going back to our physical Vault analogy earlier, let's say you've placed items in your secure vault at the bank. You visit the bank and ask to see your vault. What do you suppose the bank might ask? Your account number, name, or some other way that they can identify which vault you should have access to. You see, the bank hold 100s such vaults, all belonging to different customers. You still need your key. But knowing your identity allows them to direct you to the correct vault, the one that your key fits.

You may have multiple such vaults with the bank, each with their own unique identifier such as a number. That is the concept behind a Vault ID – a method to identify the specific vault among many and to request the relevant key or passphrase for access.

Ansible vault supports Vault IDs. They are powerful. They allow you to have multiple different identities, each with their own passphrase, enabling you to separate concerns within your Ansible playbooks. That is useful for a variety of reasons:

1. Access control – You may have some areas of the system that use shared secrets, such as a test environment or an error-reporting API service. Many developers on the team will likely have access to such credentials while not requiring access to the company's website TLS keys which are only deployed by a small subset of developers.

2. Environment separation – Knowing that you can't possibly be deploying production credentials to your test system can be reassuring, especially where the security posture of the two systems is vastly different, as is often the case.

With this in mind, we recommend always using a vault-id with your Ansible vaults – even when you only have one. It allows you to extend your playbooks and environments later, without having to refactor your existing vaults, configuration files, deployment tooling, and developer instructions.

The way to specify a Vault ID is simple. You can name it anything you like, so let's start with "example." You also need to specify how you will pass the Vault ID into the program. This can be one of

1. Prompt – Ansible will prompt you for the password at runtime. This is the method we will use most often, as it does not require us to store the vault password anywhere on disk.

2. Filename – Ansible will open the filename provided and use the contents as the Vault ID password. This can be useful when automating ansible playbook runs, but care needs to be taken that this file is not written to a disk for security reasons.

3. Script name – Ansible can execute a script to locate the Vault ID password. This allows integration with key management systems, remote APIs, or anything else you might script up. This is an advanced use case, requiring development effort.

The way to create an Ansible vault, as we did earlier, this time using a Vault ID, is simple. It combines the preceding elements:

```
$ ansible-vault create --vault-id example@prompt my_vaultid.yml
New vault password (example): mypassword
Confirm new vault password (example): mypassword
```

The order of the parameters passed to the ansible-vault command is important. The action (create, decrypt, rekey, etc.) must appear before --vault-id and finally the filename.

You'll notice that this process is almost identical as previously, with one notable exception. This time, the label example appears when ansible-vault requests you to enter a password. That is the prompt for the Vault ID name. That's your vault identifier for the bank, and the password is your key.

View the contents of the vault file, using the cat command as we did earlier:

```
$ cat my_vaultid.yml
$ANSIBLE_VAULT;1.2;AES256;example
363935303433643461623936303462626634663037353133337346531343439
3065336131643934 31
62343366353164333661343336613366353632386437353360a373363326432
343736343565326366
```

66386138363737326663336332326430623131376637643334643331613331
303939383134646666
333961316266313635 0a6135396661323031623438323838323431306437
653439626339396132
3130

Notice that there is now an additional field in the header line.
Following AES-256, we now see the vault-id label example. That is how
Ansible knows which label to use when looking for the relevant vault-id
password.

Now let's view the contents of the vault, the same as we did earlier, this
time passing our new Vault ID:

```
$ ansible-vault view --vault-id example@prompt my_vaultid.yml
Vault password (example): mypassword [enter]
```

Again, the vault-id appears in the prompt. This is important. Once
you are using multiple vault-ids, Ansible will prompt you for each one.
The label is how you'll know which password to provide. For example, it
is quite possible to experience multiple vault ID prompts when running a
playbook:

```
Vault password (shared): mypassword
Vault password (webserver): mypassword
Vault password (database): mypassword
```

Encrypting Secrets

A word of caution about decryption: We do not use the decrypt function of ansible-vault. When running decrypt, the encrypted contents of your vault are decrypted and **stored in plaintext** on the disk, under the original filename. This is something we almost never want.

Configuration Files

We will come back to, and use, ansible vault files shortly; but first let's explore another feature of ansible-vault which may well be the one we use more than any other: encrypt_string.

The power behind this simple command is immense. Take, for example, the following two configuration files of identical contents. The first is using an ansible vault file, and the latter is using encrypt_string:

```
> cat credentials_vault.yml
```

```
$ANSIBLE_VAULT;1.1;AES256;example
30656166646630313631356235636538336433333138366363663366363037
65623065396365613536633832343663339623438386334336635566303435
38320a63333353639666163306613937643264636136613333363333462373039
38306531663930653933393236343863356539316361316332306632353537
64393463650a383164636332626133386313533356663613236373533353965
66643139383137323666616263356138656633633865323861656233663164
61333832663263383393031653865373231353534646463383861613353333
663030376533323764
```

```
> cat credentials.yml
```

```
username: admin
password: !vault |
          $ANSIBLE_VAULT;1.1;AES256;example
```
65633266653533626262313536356232306261386232613732653531313065
39633365383164653564303837353934646661633863336634323765326663
61650a35646234353831666330306565613437613665646564643034613136
65633465393066653934353336563306336323562306233663363643737626166
31376331340a31636463337653462613432376562666436393462613264313 8
64656534313030
```

Believe it or not, these two files contain identical contents. They both contain the admin username and password for a fictitious system. The important thing to note is that the encrypt_string version enables us to view the variable names and contents, with only the sensitive parts encrypted – the password itself.

Why does this matter? Well, picture the scenario. You've inherited a codebase that is reaching 1000s of files large; there are 10,000 lines of Ansible code, variables, configuration files, and secrets. You have references throughout your Ansible code to magic variable names that seemingly don't exist. You see, they are locked away along with their corresponding values, encrypted in ansible vault files.

You are debugging a production issue. The variable name is nowhere to be found because the previous developer gave away no hints, naming it simply "password." True story! Where to start?

1.  git grep is of no help; the variable name is encrypted.

2.  Manually looking through vault names won't help; you have no context to link to them.

3.  All that's left is to start hunting, vault after vault, hoping you can find a single variable named "password."
```

To prevent this scenario, there are broadly two avenues:

1. Semantic variable naming, for example, VAULT_
   DB_PASSWORD to express that the password is
   contained in the vault named db. This can quickly
   descend into chaos if Vaults aren't named very
   carefully. Renaming a vault can entail large refactors
   across the codebase.

2. encrypt_string – Leaving the keys in plaintext,
   rendering git grep awesome again, and only
   encrypting the sensitive value.

Enter encrypt_string.

Encrypting Your Credentials

Let's look back at our database credentials. We made the rookie mistake
of storing these in plaintext – something we will never, ever do again after
reading this chapter, right?

Let's review the file inventory/group_vars/all:

```
---
http_port: 80
https_port: 443

database:
    host: db-001.local
    name: wordpress
    username: wordpress_rw
    password: SomeSuperStrongPassword
    root_password: EvenStrongerPassword
```

Clearly, these passwords are not very strong at all, but ignoring that, they are also stored in plaintext. Let's convert them into encrypted strings using the `ansible-vault encrypt_string` feature while preserving the all-important context in which they are used.

We launch the `encrypt_string` function without passing a string. This ensures that the secret that we are encrypting will not appear in our command history (try typing `history` if you're not familiar). When launched in this way, ansible-vault will request the string to encrypt, which is much more secure.

Enter the details as shown in bold in the following. Commands in square brackets signify a key combination to press, such as enter or ctrl-d:

> **ansible-vault encrypt_string --vault-id example@prompt**
New vault password (example): **test [enter]**
Confirm new vault password (example): **test [enter]**
Reading plaintext input from stdin. (ctrl-d to end input)
SomeSuperStrongPassword
[ctrl-d]

!vault |
        $ANSIBLE_VAULT;1.1;AES256;example
3639613037343133338636534353636633735326130663764636439303233533
3233393665393233656161613462623761863393532
Encryption successful

What just happened? `encrypt_string` took in two inputs: the password that you want to use to encrypt the string and the plaintext string that should be encrypted. It then output a specially formatted encrypted string that contains all the information needed for Ansible to decrypt this as a vault. This string is identical to a Vault file.

You can now copy this entire string and replace the previous database password in the configuration file so that it looks like this:

```
---
http_port: 80
https_port: 443

database:
    host: db-001.local
    name: wordpress
    username: wordpress_rw
    password: !vault |
        $ANSIBLE_VAULT;1.1;AES256
36396130373431333386365343536366337353261306637646364393030323533
32333936653932336561616134626237613863393532323837343164356363
33300a3264353765393162633773635616531303838326630376231346564437
39306636656562353036653838616336646538383839613266232313564538
38663735660a3034366362636316634353032336130633531316536336613765
33636337316437633938376265373436393662383361326535356161393139
3230313564663539
        root_password: EvenStrongerPassword
```

Try repeating the preceding commands to also replace the value for root_password before we attempt to run our Ansible playbooks again.

Note   It is important that you use the same vault password for all vault files using the same vault-id; otherwise, Ansible will be unable to decrypt them successfully.

Rerun the Playbook

Before we run the playbook, we must tell Ansible that we are using vaults and where to find the vault-id password. When ansible first encounters a variable with an encrypted string, it will automatically attempt to decrypt the value; however, if we do not pass it the correct secret, then it will fail.

To do this, we can use the command-line option --vault-id again, which tells Ansible to ask for the relevant vault password before running the playbook:

```
> ansible-playbook --vault-id example@prompt provision.yml
--limit databases
Vault password (example): [ctrl-c]
```

Note   The special key combination ctrl-c cancels the current command, returning us to the command prompt. We do not yet want to execute the Ansible playbook.

As Vault files are a central component of our playbooks, this password will be needed for every run. We can add a line to the ansible.cfg file to ensure it is always requested:

ansible.cfg:

```
[defaults]
inventory = inventory
stdout_callback = yaml
host_key_checking = false
vault_identity_list = example@prompt
```

Now, we can execute the playbook without the `--vault-id` parameter. Ansible will automatically know to obtain the password for the Vault ID example via a prompt:

```
ansible-playbook provision.yml --limit databases
Vault password (example): test [enter]
```

Add SSL to Our Load Balancer

We will now add SSL to our WordPress website. This requires storage of a private key, which is highly sensitive – possession of this key enables a website to impersonate your service. It is your proof of identity to your website visitors. As such, it must be kept under lock and key.

First, we must generate the SSL key. For this purpose, we will use something known as a self-signed certificate. That means it is not signed by a trusted certificate authority, but simply by yourself. The web browser will recognize that and issue a warning as it does not have the same assertions as a certificate authority issued certificate. That is ok for our example website, but not for a production one.

To do so, on the controller virtual machine

```
> openssl req -x509 -nodes -subj=/CN=lb-001.local -keyout
website.key -out website.crt

Generating a RSA private key
.....................................................+++++
..............+++++
writing new private key to 'website.key'
-----
```

Don't worry too much about the syntax of this command; it is outside the scope of this book. Essentially, we are generating a self-signed SSL certificate using a common name of lb-001.local to match our load balancer's hostname.

This will result in two files being created:

1. website.crt – The public certificate for the website. This is not sensitive and can be shared broadly, so there is no need to protect it with a vault.

2. website.key – The private key. This needs to be deployed to our load balancer. It is sensitive and needs protecting since it allows anybody with access to impersonate our trusted web server.

The preceding command results in the private key being stored unencrypted on disk. That is not something we would generally do, but for the purposes of our self-signed test system, it is a reasonable trade-off. Normally, one would receive this key from a certificate authority and handle it with the sensitivity it deserves.

HAProxy, the application we use for our load balancer, requires these files to be in a single file known as a PEM file. To achieve this, we simply concatenate (merge) the two files into one:

```
> cat website.crt website.key > website.pem
```

We will encrypt this new PEM file directly, resulting in a whole file Vault. This will then be moved into the relevant role and deployed using the copy module within the ansible playbook. We'll use a second Vault ID for this, to demonstrate how multiple Vault IDs work.

Let's do that now:

```
$ ansible-vault encrypt --vault-id website@prompt --encrypt-
vault-id website website.pem
```

```
New vault password (example): test [enter]
Confirm new vault password (example): test [enter]
New vault password (website): test [enter]
Confirm new vault password (website): test [enter]
Encryption successful
```

You are prompted for the example vault ID password here, because
we previously configured it as a default inside our ansible.cfg file.
The vault ID used for encryption is that provided to --encrypt-
vault-id.

Congratulations, your private key is now encrypted inside an Ansible
Vault with the Vault ID website. Let's add this new Vault ID to the list of
those requested when executing our playbooks.

Edit ansible.cfg and add as follows:

```
[defaults]
inventory = inventory
stdout_callback = yaml
host_key_checking = false
vault_identity_list = example@prompt, website@prompt
```

It's now time to deploy the certificate and private key to the load
balancer using Ansible playbooks. First, move the files into the role:

```
> mkdir roles/load_balancer/files/
> mv website.pem roles/load_balancer/files/
```

Then modify the playbook role load_balancer tasks:

roles/load_balancer/tasks/main.yml

```
---
- name: Install HAProxy
  apt:
    name: haproxy
    state: present

- name: Ensure SSL certificate is installed
  copy:
    src: website.pem
    dest: /etc/ssl/
```

<truncated>

This will result in the SSL PEM certificate/key being copied to the /etc/ssl/ directory of the host lb-001. We now need to point our HAProxy configuration file at this SSL certificate for it to be used by a new HTTPS endpoint for the WordPress website. Modify the templates/frontends.cfg.j2 file from earlier to add the HTTPS endpoint:

roles/load_balancer/templates/frontends.cfg.j2:

```
frontend awesome_ansible
    bind *:{{ http_port }}
    bind *:{{ https_port }} ssl crt /etc/ssl/website.pem
    stats enable
    default_backend web_servers
```

Finally, let's rerun our playbook against the load balancer. This time, we expect to be prompted for two Vault ID passwords:

1. example – The main Vault password for our playbooks

2. website – The Vault ID used for the website's SSL certificate

```
> ansible-playbook provision.yml --limit lb-001.local

Vault password (example): test [enter]
Vault password (website): test [enter]

<truncated>
```

Visit the frontend using the new SSL certificate via a web browser. You should receive a certificate error due to the certificate being self-signed. You can safely proceed to the website (on Chrome, you need to click "Advanced" before being able to proceed). You should be presented with the WordPress website secured using SSL:

```
https://lb-001.local/wordpress/
```

Summary

In this chapter, we dived into the wonderful world of Vaults. Much like a vault at home or held with the bank, they lock away your most prized possessions (credentials, secrets) with restricted access. You need to provide the correct key to unlock the vault before you can view those possessions. We created a simple Vault, learning about the `ansible-vault` command's various actions such as encrypt, decrypt, and view. We walked through the concept of Vault IDs and multiple different Vaults for different levels of access. Even if only using a single Vault ID, it is always worth starting with them, since future development work can easily build upon what is there.

Once we had a grasp on Vault IDs, we created some inline vaults for our existing configuration file's secrets, namely, the database admin and user passwords. This shows how you can easily encrypt your various API keys, passwords, disk decryption keys, or anything that might be considered sensitive in your production systems. You can even check the Vaults into source control safely. Just guard the password well.

After having a working inline vault for our database passwords, we moved on to implementing SSL for the WordPress website we had completed in the previous chapters. This involved generating a self-signed SSL certificate and key, before encrypting it with Ansible Vault. We used a second Vault ID to show how multiple Vault IDs could be used within a single Ansible run.

Despite deploying SSL, we didn't actually use the openssl_certificate module of Ansible – for two reasons. First, we wanted to demonstrate the power of Vault files in our environment. Second, we want the SSL key to be generated once and persist between Ansible executions.

After deploying the new playbooks, our WordPress website was accessible via the load balancer using HTTPS with our self-signed certificate. And with that unlocked the potential for using Ansible vaults inline or as encrypted files, within configuration files or inside roles. This empowers you to create production-grade playbooks, without worrying that your secrets might be inadvertently exposed.

CHAPTER 13

Worlds of Possibility

Congratulations. You've created a fully functioning Wordpress website that can be repeatably deployed using Ansible. You can destroy all the infrastructure and recreate it at will using a single command. It consists of two backend web servers, a database and a load balancer. It serves your website via both HTTP and HTTPS, and your secrets are safely protected by Ansible Vaults. You have an appreciation for building inventories, managing variables and using filters, building configurations, writing templated configuration files using the powerful Jinja2, controlling the flow of execution, using tags to include or exclude tasks, building reusable roles, and securing sensitive content with vaults. That is quite a comprehensive list. You now have all the foundational knowledge to succeed in understanding existing playbooks, modifying them, and developing them from scratch by yourself.

You've used some of the common core modules from Ansible to provision and manage your servers. The skills you have used to build this are very transferrable, and Ansible really does offer a world of possibilities. With the foundational knowledge that you've built up throughout this book, you should be able to quickly and easily get started using many more Ansible modules, of which there are thousands, while also expanding your use of the core modules that we've worked through.

In this chapter, we'll walk through some resources that will provide useful next steps on your journey, giving a glimpse of what's possible with some useful pointers on where to go next.

© Shaun R Smith and Peter Membrey 2022
S. R. Smith and P. Membrey, *Beginning Ansible Concepts and Application*,
https://doi.org/10.1007/978-1-4842-8173-4_13

Using the Documentation

The documentation for Ansible is exemplary. It is one of the most valuable sources of information on your journey extending your Ansible knowledge and skills.

You'll find this documentation at docs.ansible.com/ansible and via the command-line tool: `ansible-doc`.

Website Community Documentation

We recommend using the community documentation to discover which Ansible modules exist and how to use them. A great place to start would be the "Collection Index" at `https://docs.ansible.com/ansible/latest/collections/`

Here, you will find a list of module collections, or categories, that group related modules together. For example, were you using Amazon AWS extensively and wanted to manage this infrastructure via your Ansible playbooks, you will find the `amazon.aws` collection.

This collection contains a variety of Ansible modules for the various services offered by AWS; some examples include

ec2 – Create, terminate, and manage the life cycle for EC2 instances

ec2_elb – Manage AWS Elastic Load Balancer provisioning

s3_bucket – Create, manage, and destroy S3 buckets across multiple cloud provider platforms

Another great way to find modules would be using the search box, especially if you already know the name of the module that you're looking for. For example, we've touched on the `template` module in this book.

There are many more options available for that module, such as setting ownership and permissions of the resulting file(s), overwriting changes, how newlines are written, etc.

The ansible-doc Tool

Alternatively, you may find yourself working on Ansible playbooks via a terminal. In that case, you may prefer to look up documentation directly from the terminal. This is like using man pages.

To find documentation for a specific module, in this case we will look at the haproxy module. This is relevant to us, as we've just built a HAProxy load balancer. Let's use ansible-doc to find out how we might use this module:

```
> ansible-doc haproxy
```

This will present you with the full documentation page, as it would appear on docs.ansible.com, explaining

1. What the module does

2. The options the module accepts and the impact they have

3. Notes

4. Author information

5. Examples

Pay attention to the examples section. They are thorough and well documented. It is quite possibly the quickest and easiest way to understand the use cases for a given module and how you might get up and running in your environment.

Ansible Galaxy

Ansible Galaxy can form a huge part of your playbook-writing experience. Galaxy provides premade packing cubes (roles) and collections that extend those provided by Ansible, for use in your own playbooks. You came across the term collection in the Ansible documentation earlier in this chapter. A collection can provide you with new inventory sources, additional modules, and multiple roles and playbooks, making them very powerful. In fact, we discussed some collections previously: `amazon.aws` is a collection that is available via Ansible Galaxy; see `https://galaxy.ansible.com/amazon/aws`.

Some collections are installed alongside the Ansible package. Those you will find on docs.ansible.com. However, there are many thousands more available via Ansible Galaxy, which can be installed and used with ease.

To see a list of collections currently installed:

```
ansible-galaxy collection list
```

In this list, you'll likely (depending on how Ansible was installed) see many collections matching those you previously browsed on the Ansible documentation website, such as `amazon.aws`. These are installed by default and ready to use within your playbooks.

To install a new collection via Ansible Galaxy, you'll first need to search through the available collections at galaxy.ansible.com – there are literally 10,000s available. We recommend using those from reputable sources, with a large number of downloads. First, find a collection that solves your need. For this example, we will use `onepassword.connect`. This collection provides modules and plugins to interact directly with 1password from Ansible. This can be useful to store generated passwords or to retrieve passwords to deploy to services in an automated fashion. To install, simply

```
ansible-galaxy collection install onepassword.connect
```

You can now use the collection's modules, plugins, and roles within your ansible playbooks, as you would for any of the built-in or preprovided collections that came along with Ansible. One thing to note is that you should refer to the collection by its fully qualified name. That consists of <namespace>.<name>.<module>. For example, when using the modules provided by onepassword.connect, the namespace is onepassword. The name is connect, and the module is generic_item for creation or item_info for retrieval.

With that in mind, here is how we would create a new password:

```
- name: Create a new password in 1password
  onepassword.connect.generic_item:
      vault_id: "some_vault_id"
      title: "My super secret password"
      state: present
      fields:
        - label: Password
          value: "MySuperSecurePassword"
          field_type: conealed
      no_log: true
```

For repeated use of these modules throughout the playbook, you may wish to "import" the collection's namespace into your playbook. You can use only the module's name to invoke the module, such as generic_item. To do so, add a YAML list called collections: before defining the tasks, for example:

```
- hosts: all
  collections:
      - onepassword.connect
  tasks:
    - name: Create a new password in 1password
      generic_item:
        <etc>
```

Useful Collections

As you may be realizing, there is a huge wealth of modules, roles, and plugins available for Ansible, allowing you to achieve almost anything your heart desires. We almost never need to solve a problem that hasn't already been packaged up into a neat collection for our use – which is great news when getting infrastructure up and running.

In Table 13-1, we list some common collections that you might find interesting in the hopes it will kick-start your deep dive into the world of configuration management.

Table 13-1. *Useful Ansible Collections*

Name	Detail
community. crypto	Create, modify, and revoke various types of cryptographic keys such as SSH, OpenSSL, and LUKS encryption
amazon.aws	A range of plugins to provide inventory sources and lookups, along with modules to manage all manner of AWS resources such as ELB, VPC, S3, etc.
azure. azcollection	Similar to AWS but for Microsoft Azure
google.cloud	Similar to AWS but for Google Cloud
cisco.*	Modules for managing configuration of all manner of Cisco devices, including ASA, IOS, NXOS
community. grafana	Plugins and modules to interact with Grafana dashboards, users, and teams. Provides the ability to send Ansible events as chart annotations
kubernetes. core	Plugins to enable K8s as an inventory source for Ansible, query the APIs, and manage clusters and objects

(*continued*)

Table 13-1. (*continued*)

Name	Detail
community. docker	Manage docker images, networks, volumes, and containers, along with docker-swarm nodes via Ansible
community. mysql	Create and manage MySQL databases, user grants, replication, and configuration
community. postgresql	Similar to MySQL but for PostgreSQL
community. windows	A collection of modules for managing Windows nodes including Active Directory, DHCP, IIS, Disk Management, and much more

Getting Help

Ansible error messages are usually quite comprehensive and self-explanatory. Throughout this book, we have introduced you to some common errors and resolved them through the exercises. In this section, we want to provide some pointers as to where to get help when you're stuck.

Documentation

The first place to being would, of course, be the extensive documentation that we touched on earlier in this chapter. The starting point for documentation is docs.ansible.com.

Mailing Lists

Second, Ansible has a busy and helpful mailing list over on Google Groups: http://groups.google.com/group/ansible-project.

Some important tips for requesting help from this mailing list. Initially, you should search to see if a similar question has been answered previously. There is a huge amount of historical content, and it is unlikely that you're the first to hit the problem you are currently facing. You should also ensure that you are running the latest stable version of Ansible (see `ansible --version`). It is quite possible that if your problem is caused by a bug in the Ansible software, then it may already have been reported and fixed in the latest version.

Once you've confirmed that your question has not been answered before and that it reproduces with the latest release of Ansible, it's time to post your question. Include as much detail as possible. This allows others to follow along with the steps taken that got you where you are. You should include what you are trying to achieve, the commands that you ran, the full output from those commands, and importantly the operating system, environment, and version of Ansible that you are running.

Non-Ansible Resources

Of course, the usual websites for getting technical help apply. Places like Stack Overflow (`www.stackoverflow.com`) have an extensive number of questions and answers on topics related to Ansible and can be a great resource for debugging common problems. Many of these resources can be easily found with a quick search. Include the word "Ansible" and a description of the problem you're facing, and you'll likely find something useful.

Summary

This chapter walked you through the world of Ansible and its community. It provided you the resources to go out on your own and grow both the depth and breadth of your understanding. The authors genuinely believe that curiosity is the most important skill of all. So above all else, we hope that we have instilled a sense of just how powerful and extensible Ansible really is and got you hooked on the endless world of Ansible Galaxy.

We hope that we have sufficiently piqued your curiosity and provided enough of a foundation that you can confidently understand Ansible documentation and start building the blocks that make up more complex Ansible playbooks for whatever challenge comes your way.

Index

© Shaun R Smith and Peter Membrey 2022
S. R. Smith and P. Membrey, *Beginning Ansible Concepts and Application*,
https://doi.org/10.1007/978-1-4842-8173-4

Printed in the United States
by Baker & Taylor Publisher Services